DAN-11   DANTES SUBJECT STANDARDIZED TESTS (DSST)

This is your
PASSBOOK for...

Criminology (Criminal Justice)

Test Preparation Study Guide
Questions & Answers

COPYRIGHT NOTICE

This book is SOLELY intended for, is sold ONLY to, and its use is RESTRICTED to individual, bona fide applicants or candidates who qualify by virtue of having seriously filed applications for appropriate license, certificate, professional and/or promotional advancement, higher school matriculation, scholarship, or other legitimate requirements of education and/or governmental authorities.

This book is NOT intended for use, class instruction, tutoring, training, duplication, copying, reprinting, excerption, or adaptation, etc., by:

1) Other publishers
2) Proprietors and/or Instructors of "Coaching" and/or Preparatory Courses
3) Personnel and/or Training Divisions of commercial, industrial, and governmental organizations
4) Schools, colleges, or universities and/or their departments and staffs, including teachers and other personnel
5) Testing Agencies or Bureaus
6) Study groups which seek by the purchase of a single volume to copy and/or duplicate and/or adapt this material for use by the group as a whole without having purchased individual volumes for each of the members of the group
7) Et al.

Such persons would be in violation of appropriate Federal and State statutes.

PROVISION OF LICENSING AGREEMENTS – Recognized educational, commercial, industrial, and governmental institutions and organizations, and others legitimately engaged in educational pursuits, including training, testing, and measurement activities, may address request for a licensing agreement to the copyright owners, who will determine whether, and under what conditions, including fees and charges, the materials in this book may be used them. In other words, a licensing facility exists for the legitimate use of the material in this book on other than an individual basis. However, it is asseverated and affirmed here that the material in this book CANNOT be used without the receipt of the express permission of such a licensing agreement from the Publishers. Inquiries re licensing should be addressed to the company, attention rights and permissions department.

All rights reserved, including the right of reproduction in whole or in part, in any form or by any means, electronic or mechanical, including photocopying, recording, or by any information storage and retrieval system, without permission in writing from the Publisher.

Copyright © 2025 by
National Learning Corporation

212 Michael Drive, Syosset, NY 11791
(516) 921-8888 • www.passbooks.com
E-mail: info@passbooks.com

PASSBOOK® SERIES

THE *PASSBOOK® SERIES* has been created to prepare applicants and candidates for the ultimate academic battlefield – the examination room.

At some time in our lives, each and every one of us may be required to take an examination – for validation, matriculation, admission, qualification, registration, certification, or licensure.

Based on the assumption that every applicant or candidate has met the basic formal educational standards, has taken the required number of courses, and read the necessary texts, the *PASSBOOK® SERIES* furnishes the one special preparation which may assure passing with confidence, instead of failing with insecurity. Examination questions – together with answers – are furnished as the basic vehicle for study so that the mysteries of the examination and its compounding difficulties may be eliminated or diminished by a sure method.

This book is meant to help you pass your examination provided that you qualify and are serious in your objective.

The entire field is reviewed through the huge store of content information which is succinctly presented through a provocative and challenging approach – the question-and-answer method.

A climate of success is established by furnishing the correct answers at the end of each test.

You soon learn to recognize types of questions, forms of questions, and patterns of questioning. You may even begin to anticipate expected outcomes.

You perceive that many questions are repeated or adapted so that you can gain acute insights, which may enable you to score many sure points.

You learn how to confront new questions, or types of questions, and to attack them confidently and work out the correct answers.

You note objectives and emphases, and recognize pitfalls and dangers, so that you may make positive educational adjustments.

Moreover, you are kept fully informed in relation to new concepts, methods, practices, and directions in the field.

You discover that you are actually taking the examination all the time: you are preparing for the examination by "taking" an examination, not by reading extraneous and/or supererogatory textbooks.

In short, this PASSBOOK®, used directedly, should be an important factor in helping you to pass your test.

NONTRADITIONAL EDUCATION

Students returning to school as adults bring more varied experience to their studies than do the teenagers who begin college shortly after graduating from high school. As a result, there are numerous programs for students with nontraditional learning curves. Hundreds of colleges and universities grant degrees to people who cannot attend classes at a regular campus or have already learned what the college is supposed to teach.

You can earn nontraditional education credits in many ways:
- Passing standardized exams
- Demonstrating knowledge gained through experience
- Completing campus-based coursework, and
- Taking courses off campus

Some methods of assessing learning for credit are objective, such as standardized tests. Others are more subjective, such as a review of life experiences.

With some help from four hypothetical characters – Alice, Vin, Lynette, and Jorge – this article describes nontraditional ways of earning educational credit. It begins by describing programs in which you can earn a high school diploma without spending 4 years in a classroom. The college picture is more complicated, so it is presented in two parts: one on gaining credit for what you know through course work or experience, and a second on college degree programs. The final section lists resources for locating more information.

Earning High School Credit

People who were prevented from finishing high school as teenagers have several options if they want to do so as adults. Some major cities have back-to-school programs that allow adults to attend high school classes with current students. But the more practical alternatives for most adults are to take the General Educational Development (GED) tests or to earn a high school diploma by demonstrating their skills or taking correspondence classes.

Of course, these options do not match the experience of staying in high school and graduating with one's friends. But they are viable alternatives for adult learners committed to meeting and, often, continuing their educational goals.

GED Program

Alice quit high school her sophomore year and took a job to help support herself, her younger brother, and their newly widowed mother. Now an adult, she wants to earn her high school diploma – and then go on to college. Because her job as head cook and her family responsibilities keep her busy during the day, she plans to get a high school equivalency diploma. She will study for, and take, the GED tests. Every year, about half a million adults earn their high school credentials this way. A GED diploma is accepted in lieu of a high school one by more than 90 percent of employers, colleges, and universities, so it is a good choice for someone like Alice.

The GED testing program is sponsored by the American Council on Education and State and local education departments. It consists of examinations in five subject areas: Writing, science, mathematics, social studies, and literature and the arts. The tests also measure skills such as analytical ability, problem solving, reading comprehension, and ability to understand and apply information. Most of the questions are multiple choice; the writing test includes an essay section on a topic of general interest.

Eligibility rules for taking the exams vary, but some states require that you must be at least 18. Tests are given in English, Spanish, and French. In addition to standard print, versions in large print, Braille, and audiocassette are also available. Total time allotted for the tests is 7 1/2 hours.

The GED tests are not easy. About one-fourth of those who complete the exams every year do not pass. Passing scores are established by administering the tests to a sample of graduating high school seniors. The minimum standard score is set so that about one-third of graduating seniors would not pass the tests if they took them.

Because of the difficulty of the tests, people need to prepare themselves to take them. Often, they start by taking the Official GED Practice Tests, usually available through a local adult education center. Centers are listed in your phone book's blue pages under "Adult Education," "Continuing Education," or "GED." Adult education centers also have information about GED preparation classes and self-study materials. Classes are generally arranged to accommodate adults' work schedules. National Learning Corporation publishes several study guides that aim to thoroughly prepare test-takers for the GED.

School districts, colleges, adult education centers, and community organizations have information about GED testing schedules and practice tests. For more information, contact them, your nearest GED testing center, or:

GED Testing Service
One Dupont Circle, NW, Suite 250
Washington, DC 20036-1163
1(800) 62-MY GED (626-9433)
(202) 939-9490

Skills Demonstration

Adults who have acquired high school level skills through experience might be eligible for the National External Diploma Program. This alternative to the GED does not involve any direct instruction. Instead, adults seeking a high school diploma must demonstrate mastery of 65 competencies in 8 general areas: Communication; computation; occupational preparedness; and self, social, consumer, scientific, and technological awareness.

Mastery is shown through the completion of the tasks. For example, a participant could prove competency in computation by measuring a room for carpeting, figuring out the amount of carpet needed, and computing the cost.

Before being accepted for the program, adults undergo an evaluation. Tests taken at one of the program's offices measure reading, writing, and mathematics abilities. A take-home segment includes a self-assessment of current skills, an individual skill evaluation, and an occupational interest and aptitude test.

Adults accepted for the program have weekly meetings with an assessor. At the meeting, the assessor reviews the participant's work from the previous week. If the task has not been completed properly, the assessor explains the mistake. Participants continue to correct their errors until they master each competency. A high school diploma is awarded upon proven mastery of all 65 competencies.

Fourteen States and the District of Columbia now offer the External Diploma Program. For more information, contact:
External Diploma Program
One Dupont Circle, NW, Suite 250
Washington, DC 20036-1193
(202) 939-9475

Correspondence and Distance Study
Vin dropped out of high school during his junior year because his family's frequent moves made it difficult for him to continue his studies. He promised himself at the time he dropped out that he would someday finish the courses needed for his diploma. For people like Vin, who prefer to earn a traditional diploma in a nontraditional way, there are about a dozen accredited courses of study for earning a high school diploma by correspondence, or distance study. The programs are either privately run, affiliated with a university, or administered by a State education department.

Distance study diploma programs have no residency requirements, allowing students to continue their studies from almost any location. Depending on the course of study, students need not be enrolled full time and usually have more flexible schedules for finishing their work. Selection of courses ranges from vo-tech to college prep, and some programs place different emphasis on the types of diplomas offered. University affiliated schools, for example, allow qualified students to take college courses along with their high school ones. Students can then apply the college credits toward a degree at that university or transfer them to another institution.

Taking courses by distance study is often more challenging and time consuming than attending classes, especially for adults who have other obligations. Success depends on each student's motivation. Students usually do reading assignments on their own. Written exercises, which they complete and send to an instructor for grading, supplement their reading material.

A list of some accredited high schools that offer diplomas by distance study is available free from the Distance Education and Training Council, formerly known as the National Home Study Council. Request the "DETC Directory of Accredited Institutions" from:
The Distance Education and Training Council
1601 18th Street, NW.
Washington, DC 20009-2529
(202) 234-5100

Some publications profiling nontraditional college programs include addresses and descriptions of several high school correspondence ones. See the Resources section at the end of this article for more information.

Getting College Credit For What You Know
Adults can receive college credit for prior coursework, by passing examinations, and documenting experiential learning. With help from a college advisor, nontraditional students should assess their skills, establish their educational goals, and determine the number of college credits they might be eligible for.

Even before you meet with a college advisor, you should collect all your school and training records. Then, make a list of all knowledge and abilities acquired through experience, no matter how irrelevant they seem to your chosen field. Next, determine your educational goals: What specific field do you wish to study? What kind of a degree do you want? Finally, determine how your past work fits into the field of study. Later on, you will evaluate educational programs to find one that's right for you.

People who have complex educational or experiential learning histories might want to have their learning evaluated by the Regents Credit Bank. The Credit Bank, operated by Regents College of the University of the State of New York, allows people to consolidate credits earned through college, experience, or other methods. Special assessments are available for Regents College enrollees whose knowledge in a specific field cannot be adequately evaluated by standardized exams. For more information, contact the Regents Credit Bank at:

Regents College
7 Columbia Circle
Albany, NY 12203-5159
(518) 464-8500

Credit For Prior College Coursework

When Lynette was in college during the 1970s, she attended several different schools and took a variety of courses. She did well in some classes and poorly in others. Now that she is a successful business owner and has more focus, Lynette thinks she should forget about her previous coursework and start from scratch. Instead, she should start from where she is.

Lynette should have all her transcripts sent to the colleges or universities of her choice and let an admissions officer determine which classes are applicable toward a degree. A few credits here and there may not seem like much, but they add up. Even if the subjects do not seem relevant to any major, they might be counted as elective credits toward a degree. And comparing the cost of transcripts with the cost of college courses, it makes sense to spend a few dollars per transcript for a chance to save hundreds, and perhaps thousands, of dollars in books and tuition.

Rules for transferring credits apply to all prior coursework at accredited colleges and universities, whether done on campus or off. Courses completed off campus, often called extended learning, include those available to students through independent study and correspondence. Many schools have extended learning programs; Brigham Young University, for example, offers more than 300 courses through its Department of Independent Study. One type of extended learning is distance learning, a form of correspondence study by technological means such as television, video and audio, CD-ROM, electronic mail, and computer tutorials. See the Resources section at the end of this article for more information about publications available from the National University Continuing Education Association.

Any previously earned college credits should be considered for transfer, no matter what the subject or the grade received. Many schools do not accept the transfer of courses graded below a C or ones taken more than a designated number of years ago. Some colleges and universities also have limits on the number of credits that can be transferred and applied toward a degree. But not all do. For example, Thomas Edison State College, New Jersey's State college for adults, accepts the transfer of all 120 hours of credit required for a baccalaureate degree – provided all the credits are transferred from regionally accredited schools, no more than 80 are at the junior college level, and the student's grades overall and in the field of study average out to C.

To assign credit for prior coursework, most schools require original transcripts. This means you must complete a form or send a written, signed request to have your transcripts released directly to a college or university. Once you have chosen the schools you want to apply to, contact the schools you attended before. Find out how much each transcript costs, and ask them to send your transcripts to the ones you are applying to. Write a letter that includes your name (and names used during attendance, if different) and dates of attendance, along with the names and addresses of the schools to which your transcripts should be sent. Include payment and mail to the registrar at the schools you have attended. The registrar's office will process your request and send an official transcript of your coursework to the colleges or universities you have designated.

Credit For Noncollege Courses

Colleges and universities are not the only ones that offer classes. Volunteer organizations and employers often provide formal training worth college credit. The American Council on Education has two programs that assess thousands of specific courses and make recommendations on the amount of college credit they are worth. Colleges and universities accept the recommendations or use them as guidelines.

One program evaluates educational courses sponsored by government agencies, business and industry, labor unions, and professional and voluntary organizations. It is the Program on Noncollegiate Sponsored Instruction (PONSI). Some of the training seminars Alice has participated in covered topics such as food preparation, kitchen safety, and nutrition. Although she has not yet earned her GED, Alice can earn college credit because of her completion of these formal job-training seminars. The number of credits each seminar is worth does not hinge on Alice's current eligibility for college enrollment.

The other program evaluates courses offered by the Army, Navy, Air Force, Marines, Coast Guard, and Department of Defense. It is the Military Evaluations Program. Jorge has never attended college, but the engineering technology classes he completed as part of his military training are worth college credit. And as an Army veteran, Jorge is eligible for a service that takes the evaluations one step further. The Army/American Council on Education Registry Transcript System (AARTS) will provide Jorge with an individualized transcript of American Council on Education credit recommendations for all courses he completed, the military occupational specialties (MOS's) he held, and examinations he passed while in the Army. All Army and National Guard enlisted personnel and veterans who enlisted after October 1981 are eligible for the transcript. Similar services are being considered by the Navy and Marine Corps.

To obtain a free transcript, see your Army Education Center for a 5454R transcript request form. Include your name, Social Security number, basic active service date, and complete address where you want the transcript sent. Mail your request to:
    AARTS Operations Center
    415 McPherson Ave.
    Fort Leavenworth, KS 66027-1373

Recommendations for PONSI are published in *The National Guide to Educational Credit for Training Programs;* military program recommendations are in *The Guide to the Evaluation of Educational Experiences in the Armed Forces.* See the Resources section at the end of this article for more information about these publications.

Former military personnel who took a foreign language course through the Defense Language Institute may request course transcripts by sending their name, Social Security number, course title, duration of the course, and graduation date to:

Commandant, Defense Language Institute
Attn: ATFL-DAA-AR
Transcripts
Presidio of Monterey
Monterey, CA 93944-5006

Not all of Jorge's and Alice's courses have been assessed by the American Council on Education. Training courses that have no Council credit recommendation should still be assessed by an advisor at the schools they want to attend. Course descriptions, class notes, test scores, and other documentation may be helpful for comparing training courses to their college equivalents. An oral examination or other demonstration of competency might also be required.

There is no guarantee you will receive all the credits you are seeking – but you certainly won't if you make no attempt.

Credit By Examination

Standardized tests are the best-known method of receiving college credit without taking courses. These exams are often taken by high school students seeking advanced placement for college, but they are also available to adult learners. Testing programs and colleges and universities offer exams in a number of subjects. Two U.S. Government institutes have foreign language exams for employees that also may be worth college credit.

It is important to understand that receiving a passing score on these exams does not mean you get college credit automatically. Each school determines which test results it will accept, minimum scores required, how scores are converted for credit, and the amount of credit, if any, to be assigned. Most colleges and universities accept the American Council on Education credit recommendations, published every other year in the 250-page *Guide to Educational Credit by Examination*. For more information, contact:

The American Council on Education
Credit by Examination Program
One Dupont Circle, Suite 250
Washington, DC 20036-1193
(202) 939-9434

Testing programs:

You might know some of the five national testing programs by their acronyms or initials: CLEP, ACT PEP: RCE, DANTES, AP, and NOCTI. (The meanings of these initialisms are explained below.) There is some overlap among programs; for example, four of them have introductory accounting exams. Since you will not be awarded credit more than once for a specific subject, you should carefully evaluate each program for the subject exams you wish to take. And before taking an exam, make sure you will be awarded credit by the college or university you plan to attend.

CLEP (College-Level Examination Program), administered by the College Board, is the most widely accepted of the national testing programs; more than 2,800 accredited schools award credit for passing exam scores. Each test covers material taught in basic undergraduate courses. There are five general exams – English composition, humanities, college mathematics, natural sciences, and social sciences and history – and many subject exams. Most exams are entirely multiple-choice, but English composition exams may include an essay section. For more information, contact:

    CLEP
    P.O. Box 6600
    Princeton, NJ 08541-6600
    (609) 771-7865

ACT PEP: RCE (American College Testing Proficiency Exam Program: Regents College Examinations) tests are given in 38 subjects within arts and sciences, business, education, and nursing. Each exam is recommended for either lower- or upper-level credit. Exams contain either objective or extended response questions, and are graded according to a standard score, letter grade, or pass/fail. Fees vary, depending on the subject and type of exam. For more information or to request free study guides, contact:

    ACT PEP: Regents College Examinations
    P.O. Box 4014
    Iowa City, IA 52243
    (319) 337-1387
    (New York State residents must contact Regents College directly.)

DANTES (Defense Activity for Nontraditional Education Support) standardized tests are developed by the Educational Testing Service for the Department of Defense. Originally administered only to military personnel, the exams have been available to the public since 1983. About 50 subject tests cover business, mathematics, social science, physical science, humanities, foreign languages, and applied technology. Most of the tests consist entirely of multiple-choice questions. Schools determine their own administering fees and testing schedules. For more information or to request free study sheets, contact:

    DANTES Program Office
    Mail Stop 31-X
    Educational Testing Service
    Princeton, NJ 08541
    1(800) 257-9484

The AP (Advanced Placement) Program is a cooperative effort between secondary schools and colleges and universities. AP exams are developed each year by committees of college and high school faculty appointed by the College Board and assisted by consultants from the Educational Testing Service. Subjects include arts and languages, natural sciences, computer science, social sciences, history, and mathematics. Most tests are 2 or 3 hours long and include both multiple-choice and essay questions. AP courses are available to help students prepare for exams, which are offered in the spring. For more information about the Advanced Placement Program, contact:

    Advanced Placement Services
    P.O. Box 6671
    Princeton, NJ 08541-6671
    (609) 771-7300

NOCTI (National Occupational Competency Testing Institute) assessments are designed for people like Alice, who have vocational-technical skills that cannot be evaluated by other tests. NOCTI assesses competency at two levels: Student/job ready and teacher/experienced worker. Standardized evaluations are available for occupations such as auto-body repair, electronics, mechanical drafting, quantity food preparation, and upholstering. The tests consist of multiple-choice questions and a performance component. Other services include workshops, customized assessments, and pre-testing. For more information, contact:

NOCTI
500 N. Bronson Ave.
Ferris State University
Big Rapids, MI 49307
(616) 796-4699

Colleges and universities:

Many colleges and universities have credit-by-exam programs, through which students earn credit by passing a comprehensive exam for a course offered by the institution. Among the most widely recognized are the programs at Ohio University, the University of North Carolina, Thomas Edison State College, and New York University.

Ohio University offers about 150 examinations for credit. In addition, you may sometimes arrange to take special examinations in non-laboratory courses offered at Ohio University. To take a test for credit, you must enroll in the course. If you plan to transfer the credit earned, you also need written permission from an official at your school. Books and study materials are available, for a cost, through the university. Exams must be taken within 6 months of the enrollment date; most last 3 hours. You may arrange to take the exam off campus if you do not live near the university.

Ohio University is on the quarter-hour system; most courses are worth 4 quarter hours, the equivalent of 3 semester hours. For more information, contact:

Independent Study
Tupper Hall 302
Ohio University
Athens, OH 45701-2979
1(800) 444-2910
(614) 593-2910

The University of North Carolina offers a credit-by-examination option for 140 independent study (correspondence) courses in foreign languages, humanities, social sciences, mathematics, business administration, education, electrical and computer engineering, health administration, and natural sciences. To take an exam, you must request and receive approval from both the course instructor and the independent studies department. Exams must be taken within six months of enrollment, and you may register for no more than two at a time. If you are not near the University's Chapel Hill campus, you may take your exam under supervision at an accredited college, university, community college, or technical institute. For more information, contact:

Independent Studies
CB #1020, The Friday Center
UNC-Chapel Hill
Chapel Hill, NC 27599-1020
1(800) 862-5669 / (919) 962-1134

The Thomas Edison College Examination Program offers more than 50 exams in liberal arts, business, and professional areas. Thomas Edison State College administers tests twice a month in Trenton, New Jersey; however, students may arrange to take their tests with a proctor at any accredited American college or university or U.S. military base. Most of the tests are multiple choice; some also include short answer or essay questions. Time limits range from 90 minutes to 4 hours, depending on the exam. For more information, contact:

Thomas Edison State College
TECEP, Office of Testing and Assessment
101 W. State Street
Trenton, NJ 08608-1176
(609) 633-2844

New York University's Foreign Language Program offers proficiency exams in more than 40 languages, from Albanian to Yiddish. Two exams are available in each language: The 12-point test is equivalent to 4 undergraduate semesters, and the 16-point exam may lead to upper level credit. The tests are given at the university's Foreign Language Department throughout the year.

Proof of foreign language proficiency does not guarantee college credit. Some colleges and universities accept transcripts only for languages commonly taught, such as French and Spanish. Nontraditional programs are more likely than traditional ones to grant credit for proficiency in other languages.

For an informational brochure and registration form for NYU's foreign language proficiency exams, contact:

New York University
Foreign Language Department
48 Cooper Square, Room 107
New York, NY 10003
(212) 998-7030

Government institutes:

The Defense Language Institute and Foreign Service Institute administer foreign language proficiency exams for personnel stationed abroad. Usually, the tests are given at the end of intensive language courses or upon completion of service overseas. But some people – like Jorge, who knows Spanish – speak another language fluently and may be allowed to take a proficiency exam in that language before completing their tour of duty. Contact one of the offices listed below to obtain transcripts of those scores. Proof of proficiency does not guarantee college credit, however, as discussed above.

To request score reports from the Defense Language Institute for Defense Language Proficiency Tests, send your name, Social Security number, language for which you were tested, and, most importantly, when and where you took the exam to:

Commandant, Defense Language Institute
Attn: ATFL-ES-T
DLPT Score Report Request
Presidio of Monterey
Monterey, CA 93944-5006

To request transcripts of scores for Foreign Service Institute exams, send your name, Social Security number, language for which you were tested, and dates or year of exams to:

Foreign Service Institute
Arlington Hall
4020 Arlington Boulevard
Rosslyn, VA 22204-1500
Attn: Testing Office (Send your request to the attention of the testing office of the foreign language in which you were tested)

Credit For Experience

Experiential learning credit may be given for knowledge gained through job responsibilities, personal hobbies, volunteer opportunities, homemaking, and other experiences. Colleges and universities base credit awards on the knowledge you have attained, not for the experience alone. In addition, the knowledge must be college level; not just any learning will do. Throwing horseshoes as a hobby is not likely to be worth college credit. But if you've done research on how and where the sport originated, visited blacksmiths, organized tournaments, and written a column for a trade journal – well, that's a horseshoe of a different color.

Adults attempting to get credit for their experience should be forewarned: Having your experience evaluated for college credit is time-consuming, tedious work – not an easy shortcut for people who want quick-fix college credits. And not all experience, no matter how valuable, is the equivalent of college courses.

Requesting college credit for your experiential learning can be tricky. You should get assistance from a credit evaluations officer at the school you plan to attend, but you should also have a general idea of what your knowledge is worth. A common method for converting knowledge into credit is to use a college catalog. Find course titles and descriptions that match what you have learned through experience, and request the number of credits offered for those courses.

Once you know what credit to ask for, you must usually present your case in writing to officials at the college you plan to attend. The most common form of presenting experiential learning for credit is the portfolio. A portfolio is a written record of your knowledge along with a request for equivalent college credit. It includes an identification and description of the knowledge for which you are requesting credit, an explanatory essay of how the knowledge was gained and how it fits into your educational plans, documentation that you have acquired such knowledge, and a request for college credit. Required elements of a portfolio vary by schools but generally follow those guidelines.

In identifying knowledge you have gained, be specific about exactly what you have learned. For example, it is not enough for Lynette to say she runs a business. She must identify the knowledge she has gained from running it, such as personnel management, tax law, marketing strategy, and inventory review. She must also include brief descriptions about her knowledge of each to support her claims of having those skills.

The essay gives you a chance to relay something about who you are. It should address your educational goals, include relevant autobiographical details, and be well organized, neat, and convey confidence. In his essay, Jorge might first state his goal of becoming an engineer. Then he would explain why he joined the Army, where he got hands-on training and experience in developing and servicing electronic equipment.

This, he would say, led to his hobby of creating remote-controlled model cars, of which he has built 20. His conclusion would highlight his accomplishments and tie them to his desire to become an electronic engineer.

Documentation is evidence that you've learned what you claim to have learned. You can show proof of knowledge in a variety of ways, including audio or video recordings, letters from current or former employers describing your specific duties and job performance, blueprints, photographs or artwork, and transcripts of certifying exams for professional licenses and certification – such as Alice's certification from the American Culinary Federation. Although documentation can take many forms, written proof alone is not always enough. If it is impossible to document your knowledge in writing, find out if your experiential learning can be assessed through supplemental oral exams by a faculty expert.

Earning a College Degree

Nontraditional students often have work, family, and financial obligations that prevent them from quitting their jobs to attend school full time. Can they still meet their educational goals? Yes.

More than 150 accredited colleges and universities have nontraditional bachelor's degree programs that require students to spend little or no time on campus; over 300 others have nontraditional campus-based degree programs. Some of those schools, as well as most junior and community colleges, offer associate's degrees nontraditionally. Each school with a nontraditional course of study determines its own rules for awarding credit for prior coursework, exams, or experience, as discussed previously. Most have charges on top of tuition for providing these special services.

Several publications profile nontraditional degree programs; see the Resources section at the end of this article for more information. To determine which school best fits your academic profile and educational goals, first list your criteria. Then, evaluate nontraditional programs based on their accreditation, features, residency requirements, and expenses. Once you have chosen several schools to explore further, write to them for more information. Detailed explanations of school policies should help you decide which ones you want to apply to.

Get beyond the printed word – especially the glowing words each school writes about itself. Check out the schools you are considering with higher education authorities, alumni, employers, family members, and friends. If possible, visit the campus to talk to students and instructors and sit in on a few classes, even if you will be completing most or all of your work off campus. Ask school officials questions about such things as enrollment numbers, graduation rate, faculty qualifications, and confusing details about the application process or academic policies. After you have thoroughly investigated each prospective college or university, you can make an informed decision about which is right for you.

Accreditation

Accreditation is a process colleges and universities submit to voluntarily for getting their credentials. An accredited school has been investigated and visited by teams of observers and has periodic inspections by a private accrediting agency. The initial review can take two years or more.

Regional agencies accredit entire schools, and professional agencies accredit either specialized schools or departments within schools. Although there are no national accrediting standards, not just any accreditation will do. Countless "accreditation associations" have been invented by schools, many of which have no academic programs and sell phony degrees, to accredit themselves. But 6 regional and about 80 professional accrediting associations in the United States are recognized by the U.S. Department of Education or the Commission on Recognition of Postsecondary Accreditation. When checking accreditation, these are the names to look for. For more information about accreditation and accrediting agencies, contact:

Institutional Participation Oversight Service Accreditation and State Liaison Division
U.S. Department of Education
ROB 3, Room 3915
600 Independence Ave., SW
Washington, DC 20202-5244
(202) 708-7417

Because accreditation is not mandatory, lack of accreditation does not necessarily mean a school or program is bad. Some schools choose not to apply for accreditation, are in the process of applying, or have educational methods too unconventional for an accrediting association's standards. For the nontraditional student, however, earning a degree from a college or university with recognized accreditation is an especially important consideration. Although nontraditional education is becoming more widely accepted, it is not yet mainstream. Employers skeptical of a degree earned in a nontraditional manner are likely to be even less accepting of one from an unaccredited school.

Program Features

Because nontraditional students have diverse educational objectives, nontraditional schools are diverse in what they offer. Some programs are geared toward helping students organize their scattered educational credits to get a degree as quickly as possible. Others cater to those who may have specific credits or experience but need assistance in completing requirements. Whatever your educational profile, you should look for a program that works with you in obtaining your educational goals.

A few nontraditional programs have special admissions policies for adult learners like Alice, who plan to earn their GEDs but want to enroll in college in the meantime. Other features of nontraditional programs include individualized learning agreements, intensive academic counseling, cooperative learning and internship placement, and waiver of some prerequisites or other requirements – as well as college credit for prior coursework, examinations, and experiential learning, all discussed previously.

Lynette, whose primary goal is to finish her degree, wants to earn maximum credits for her business experience. She will look for programs that do not limit the number of credits awarded for equivalency exams and experiential learning. And since well-documented proof of knowledge is essential for earning experiential learning credits, Lynette should make sure the program she chooses provides assistance to students submitting a portfolio.

Jorge, on the other hand, has more credits than he needs in certain areas and is willing to forego some. To become an engineer, he must have a bachelor's degree; but because he is accustomed to hands-on learning, Jorge is interested in getting experience as he gains more technical skills. He will concentrate on finding schools with strong cooperative education, supervised fieldwork, or internship programs.

Residency Requirements

Programs are sometimes deemed nontraditional because of their residency requirements. Many people think of residency for colleges and universities in terms of tuition, with in-state students paying less than out-of-state ones. Residency also may refer to where a student lives, either on or off campus, while attending school.

But in nontraditional education, residency usually refers to how much time students must spend on campus, regardless of whether they attend classes there. In some nontraditional programs, students need not ever step foot on campus. Others require only a very short residency, such as one day or a few weeks. Many schools have standard residency requirements of several semesters but schedule classes for evenings or weekends to accommodate working adults.

Lynette, who previously took courses by independent study, prefers to earn credits by distance study. She will focus on schools that have no residency requirement. Several colleges and universities have nonresident degree completion programs for adults with some college credit. Under the direction of a faculty advisor, students devise a plan for earning their remaining credits. Methods for earning credits include independent study, distance learning, seminars, supervised fieldwork, and group study at arranged sites. Students may have to earn a certain number of credits through the degree-granting institution. But many programs allow students to take courses at accredited schools of their choice for transfer toward their degree.

Alice wants to attend lectures but has an unpredictable schedule. Her best course of action will be to seek out short residency programs that require students to attend seminars once or twice a semester. She can take courses that are televised and videotape them to watch when her schedule permits, with the seminars helping to ensure that she properly completes her coursework. Many colleges and universities with short residency requirements also permit students to earn some credits elsewhere, by whatever means the student chooses.

Some fields of study require classroom instruction. As Jorge will discover, few colleges and universities allow students to earn a bachelor's degree in engineering entirely through independent study. Nontraditional residency programs are designed to accommodate adults' daytime work schedules. Jorge should look for programs offering evening, weekend, summer, and accelerated courses.

Tuition and Other Expenses

The final decisions about which schools Alice, Jorge, and Lynette attend may hinge in large part on a single issue: Cost. And rising tuition is only part of the equation. Beginning with application fees and continuing through graduation fees, college expenses add up.

Traditional and nontraditional students have some expenses in common, such as the cost of books and other materials. Tuition might even be the same for some courses, especially for colleges and universities offering standard ones at unusual times. But for nontraditional programs, students may also pay fees for services such as credit or transcript review, evaluation, advisement, and portfolio assessment.

Students are also responsible for postage and handling or setup expenses for independent study courses, as well as for all examination and transcript fees for transferring credits. Usually, the more nontraditional the program, the more detailed the fees. Some schools charge a yearly enrollment fee rather than tuition for degree completion candidates who want their files to remain active.

Although tuition and fees might seem expensive, most educators tell you not to let money come between you and your educational goals. Talk to someone in the financial aid department of the school you plan to attend or check your library for publications about financial aid sources. The U.S. Department of Education publishes a guide to Federal aid programs such as Pell Grants, student loans, and work-study. To order the free 74-page booklet, *The Student Guide: Financial Aid from the U.S. Department of Education,* contact:

> Federal Student Aid Information Center
> P.O. Box 84
> Washington, DC 20044
> 1 (800) 4FED-AID (433-3243)

Resources

Information on how to earn a high school diploma or college degree without following the usual routes is available from several organizations and in numerous publications. Information on nontraditional graduate degree programs, available for master's through doctoral level, though not discussed in this article, can usually be obtained from the same resources that detail bachelor's degree programs.

National Learning Corporation publishes study guides for all of these exams, for both general examinations and tests in specific subject areas. To order study guides, or to browse their catalog featuring more than 5,000 titles, visit NLC online at www.passbooks.com, or contact them by phone at (800) 632-8888.

Organizations

Adult learners should always contact their local school system, community college, or university to learn about programs that are readily available. The following national organizations can also supply information:

> American Council on Education
> One Dupont Circle
> Washington, DC 20036-1193
> (202) 939-9300

Within the American Council on Education, the Center for Adult Learning and Educational Credentials administers the National External Diploma Program, the GED Program, the Program on Noncollegiate Sponsored Instruction, the Credit by Examination Program, and the Military Evaluations Program.

DANTES Subject Standardized Tests

INTRODUCTION

The DANTES (Defense Activity for Non-Traditional Education Support) subject standardized tests are comprehensive college and graduate level examinations given by the Armed Forces, colleges and graduate schools as end-of-subject course evaluation final examinations or to obtain college equivalency credits in the various subject areas tested.

The DANTES Examination Program enables students to obtain college credit for what they have learned on the job, through self-study, personal interest, correspondence courses or by any other means. It is used by colleges and universities to award college credit to students who demonstrate that they know as much as students completing an equivalent college course. It is a cost-efficient, time-saving way for students to use their knowledge to accomplish their educational goals.

Most schools accept the American Council on Education (ACE) recommendations for the minimum score required and the amount of credit awarded, but not all schools do. Be sure to check the policy regarding the score level required for credit and the number of credits to be awarded.

Not all tests are accepted by all institutions. Even when a test is accepted by an institution, it may not be acceptable for every program at that institution. Before considering testing, ascertain the acceptability of a specific test for a particular course.

Colleges and universities that administer DANTES tests may administer them to any applicant – or they may administer the tests only to students registered at their institution. Decisions about who will be allowed to test are made by the school. Students should contact the test center to determine current policies and schedules for DANTES testing.

Colleges and universities authorized to administer DANTES tests usually do so throughout the calendar year. Each school sets its own fee for test administration and establishes its own testing schedule. Contact the representative at the administering school directly to make arrangements for testing.

Checklist
For Students

- ✓ Visit **www.getcollegecredit.com** to obtain a list of tests, fact sheets, test preparation materials, participating colleges and universities, and much more.

- ✓ Contact your school advisor to confirm that the DSST you selected will fit into your curriculum.

- ✓ Consult the *DSST Candidate Information Bulletin* for answers to specific questions.

- ✓ Contact the test site to schedule your test.

- ✓ Prepare for your examination by using the fact sheet as a guide.

- ✓ Take the test.

If you would like a score report sent to your college or university, it is a good idea to bring the four-digit code with you. You must write the DSST Test Center Code for that institution on your answer sheet at the time of testing. DSST Test Center Codes are noted in the DSST Participating Colleges and Universities listing on the Web site.

If you prefer to send a score report to an institution at a later date, there is a transcript fee of $20 for each transcript ordered.

Thomson Prometric
DSST Program
2000 Lenox Drive, Third Floor
Lawrenceville, NJ 08648

Toll-free: 877-471-9860
609-895-5011

E-mail: pnj-dsst@thomson.com

MAKING A COLLEGE DEGREE WITHIN YOUR REACH

Today, there are many educational alternatives to the classroom—you can learn from your job, your reading, your independent study, and special interests you pursue. You may already have learned the subject matter covered by some college-level courses.

The DSST Program is a nationally recognized testing program that gives you the opportunity to receive college credit for learning acquired outside the traditional college classroom. Colleges and universities throughout the United States administer the program, developed by Thomson Prometric, year-round. Annually, over 90,000 DSSTs are administered to individuals who are interested in continuing their education. Take advantage of the DSST testing program; it speeds the educational process and provides the flexibility adults need, making earning a degree more feasible.

Since requirements differ from college to college, please check with the credit-awarding institution before taking a DSST. More than 1,800 colleges and universities currently award credit for DSSTs, and the number is growing every day. You can choose from 37 test titles in the areas of Social Science, Business, Mathematics, Applied Technology, Humanities, and Physical Science. A brief description of each examination is found on the pages that follow.

Reach Your Career Goals Through DSSTs

Use DSSTs to help you earn your degree, get a promotion, or simply demonstrate that you have college-level knowledge in subjects relevant to your work.

Save Time...

You don't have to sit through classes when you have previously acquired the knowledge or experience for most of what is being taught and can learn the rest yourself. You might be able to bypass introductory-level courses in subject areas you already know.

Save Money...

DSSTs save you money because the classes you bypass by earning credit through the DSST Program are classes you won't have to pay for on your way to earning your degree. You can use the money instead to take more advanced courses that can be more challenging and rewarding.

Improve Your Chances for Admission to College

Each college has its own admission policies; however, having passing scores for DSSTs on your transcript can provide strong evidence of how well you can perform at the college level.

Gain Confidence Performing at a College Level

Many adults returning to college find that lack of confidence is often the greatest hurdle to overcome. Passing a DSST demonstrates your ability to perform on a college level.

Make Up for Courses You May Have Missed
You may be ready to graduate from college and find that you are a few credits short of earning your degree. By using semester breaks, vacation time, or leisure time to study independently, you can prepare to take one or more DSSTs, fulfill your academic requirements, and graduate on time.

If You Cannot Attend Regularly Scheduled Classes...
If your lifestyle or responsibilities prevent you from attending regularly scheduled classes, you can earn your college degree from a college offering an external degree program. The DSST Program allows you to earn your degree by study and experience outside the traditional classroom.

Many colleges and universities offer external degree or distance learning programs. For additional information, contact the college you plan to attend or:
Center for Lifelong Learning
American Council on Education
One DuPont Circle NW, Suite 250
Washington, DC 20036
202-939-9475
www.acenet.edu
(Select "Center for Lifelong Learning" under "Programs & Services" for more information)

Fact Sheets
For each test, there is a Fact Sheet that outlines the topics covered by each test and includes a list of sample questions, a list of recommended references of books that would be useful for review, and the number of credits awarded for a passing score as recommended by the American Council on Education (ACE). *Please note that some schools require scores that are higher than the minimum ACE-recommended passing score.* It is suggested that you check with your college or university to determine what score they require in order to earn credit. You can obtain Fact Sheets by:
- Downloading them from www.getcollegecredit.com
- E-mailing a request to pnj-dsst@thomson.com
- Completing a Candidate Publications Order Form

DSST Online Practice Tests
DSST online practice tests contain items that reflect a *partial range of difficulty* identified in the Content Outline section on each Fact Sheet. There is an online DSST Practice Test in the following categories:
- Mathematics
- Social Science
- Business
- Physical Science
- Applied Technology
- Humanities

Although the online DSST Practice Test questions do not indicate the full range of difficulty you would find in an actual DSST test, they will help you assess your knowledge level. Each online DSST Practice Test can be purchased by visiting www.getcollegecredit.com and clicking on DSST Practice Exams.

TAKING DSST EXAMINATIONS

Earning College Credit for DSST Examinations

To find out if the college of your choice awards credit for passing DSST scores, contact the admissions office or counseling and testing office. The college can also provide information on the scores required for awarding credit, the number of credit hours awarded, and any courses that can be bypassed with satisfactory scores.

It is important that you contact the institution of your choice as early as possible since credit-awarding policies differ among colleges and universities.

Where to Take DSSTs

DSSTs are administered at colleges and universities nationwide. Each location determines the frequency and scheduling of test administrations. To obtain the most current list of participating DSST colleges and universities:
- Visit and download the information from www.getcollegecredit.com
- E-mail pnj-dsst@thomson.com

Scheduling Your Examination

Please be aware that some colleges and universities provide DSST testing services to enrolled students only. After you have selected a college or university that administers DSSTs, you will need to contact them to schedule your test date.

The fee to take a DSST is $60 per test. This fee entitles you to two score reports after the test is scored. One will be sent directly to you and the other will be sent to the college or university that you designate on your answer sheet. You may pay the test fee with a certified check or U.S. money order made payable to Thomson Prometric or you may charge the test fee to your Visa, MasterCard or American Express credit card. Note: The credit card statement will reflect a charge from Thomson Prometric for all DSST examinations. *(Declined credit card charges will be assessed an additional $25 processing fee.)*

In addition, the test site may also require a test administration fee for each examination, to be paid directly to the institution. Contact the test site to determine its administration fee and payment policy.

Other Testing Arrangements

If you are unable to find a participating DSST college or university in your area, you may want to contact the testing office of a local accredited college or university to determine whether a representative from that office will agree to administer the test(s) for you.

The school's representative should then contact the DSST Program at 866-794-3497 to arrange for this administration. If you are unable to locate a test site, contact Thomson Prometric for assistance at pnj-dsst@thomson.com or 866-794-3497.

Testing Accommodations for Students with Disabilities

Thomson Prometric is committed to serving test takers with disabilities by providing services and reasonable testing accommodations as set forth in the provisions of the *Americans with Disabilities Act* (ADA). If you have a disability, as prescribed by the ADA, and require special testing services or arrangements, please contact the test administrator at the test site. You will be asked to submit to the test administrator documentation of your disability and your request for special accommodations. The test administrator will then forward your documentation along with your request for testing accommodations to Thomson Prometric for approval.

Please submit your request as far in advance of your test date as possible so that the necessary accommodations can be made. Only test takers with documented disabilities are eligible for special accommodations.

On the Day of the Examination

It is important to review this information and to have the correct identification present on the day of the examination:
- Arrive on time as a courtesy to the test administrator.
- Bring a valid form of government-issued identification that includes a current photo and your signature (acceptable documents include a driver's license, passport, state-issued identification card or military identification). *Anyone who fails to present valid identification will not be allowed to test.*
- Bring several No. 2 (soft-lead) sharpened pencils with good erasers, a watch, and a black pen if you will be writing an essay.
- Do not bring books or papers.
- Do not bring an alarm watch that beeps, a telephone, or a phone beeper into the testing room.
- The use of nonprogrammable calculators, slide rules, scratch paper and/or other materials is permitted for some of the tests.

DSST SCORING POLICIES

Your DSST examination scores are reported only to you, unless you request that they be sent elsewhere. If you want your scores sent to your college, you must provide the correct DSST code number of the school on your answer sheet at the time you take the test. See the *DSST Directory of Colleges and Universities* on the Web site www.getcollegecredit.com.

If your institution is not listed, contact Thomson Prometric at 866-794-3497 to establish a code number. (Some schools may require a student to be enrolled prior to receiving a score report.)

Receiving Your Score Report

Allow approximately four weeks after testing to receive your score report.

Calling DSST Customer Service before the required four-week score processing time has elapsed will not expedite the processing of your scores. Due to privacy and security requirements, scores will not be reported to students over the telephone under any circumstance.

Scoring of Principles of Public Speaking Speeches

The speech portion of the *Principles of Public Speaking* examination will be sent to speech raters who are faculty members at accredited colleges that currently teach or have previously taught the course. Scores for the *Principles of Public Speaking* examination are available six to eight weeks from receipt by Thomson Prometric. If you take the *Principles of Public Speaking* examination and fail (either the objective, speech portion, or both), you must follow the retesting policy waiting period of six months (180 days) before retaking the entire exam.

Essays

The essays for *Ethics in America* and *Technical Writing* are <u>optional</u> and thus are not scored by raters. The essays are forwarded to the college or university that you designate, along with your score report, for their use in determining the award of credit. <u>Before taking the *Ethics in America* or *Technical Writing* examinations, check with your college or university to determine whether the essay is required.</u>

NOTE: *Principles of Public Speaking* speech topic cassette tapes and essays are kept on file at Thomson Prometric for one year from the date of administration.

How to Get Transcripts

There is a $20 fee for each transcript you request. Payment must be in the form of a certified check, U.S. money order payable to Thomson Prometric, or credit card. Personal checks and debit cards are NOT an acceptable method of payment. One transcript may include scores for one or more examinations taken. To request a transcript, download the Transcript Order Form from www.getcollegecredit.com.

DESCRIPTION OF THE DSST EXAMINATIONS

Mathematics

- **Fundamentals of College Algebra** covers mathematical concepts such as fundamental algebraic operations; linear, absolute value; quadratic equations, inequalities, radials, exponents and logarithms, factoring polynomials and graphing. The use of a nonprogrammable, handheld calculator is permitted.

- **Principles of Statistics** tests the understanding of the various topics of statistics, both qualitatively and quantitatively, and the ability to apply statistical methods to solve a variety of problems. The topics included in this test are descriptive statistics; correlation and regression; probability; chance models and sampling and tests of significance. The use of a nonprogrammable, handheld calculator is permitted.

Social Science

- **Art of the Western World** deals with the history of art during the following periods: classical; Romanesque and Gothic; early Renaissance; high Renaissance, Baroque; rococo; neoclassicism and romanticism; realism, impressionism and post-impressionism; early twentieth century; and post-World War II.

- **Western Europe Since 1945** tests the knowledge of basic facts and terms and the understanding of concepts and principles related to the areas of the historical background of the aftermath of the Second World War and rebuilding of Europe; national political systems; issues and policies in Western European societies; European institutions and processes; and Europe's relations with the rest of the world.

- **An Introduction to the Modern Middle East** emphasizes core knowledge (including geography, Judaism, Christianity, Islam, ethnicity); nineteenth-century European impact; twentieth-century Western influences; World Wars I and II; new nations; social and cultural changes (1900-1960) and the Middle East from 1960 to present.

- **Human/Cultural Geography** includes the Earth and basic facts (coordinate systems, maps, physiography, atmosphere, soils and vegetation, water); culture and environment, spatial processes (social processes, modern economic systems, settlement patterns, political geography); and regional geography.

- **Rise and Fall of the Soviet Union** covers Russia under the Old Regime; the Revolutionary Period; New Economic Policy; Pre-war Stalinism; The Second World War; Post-war Stalinism; The Khrushchev Years; The Brezhnev Era; and reform and collapse.

- **A History of the Vietnam War** covers the history of the roots of the Vietnam War; the First Vietnam War (1946-1954); pre-war developments (1954-1963); American involvement in the Vietnam War; Tet (1968); Vietnamizing the War (1968-1973); Cambodia and Laos; peace; legacies and lessons.

- **The Civil War and Reconstruction** covers the Civil War from presecession (1861) through Reconstruction. It includes causes of the war; secession; Fort Sumter; the war in the east and in the west; major battles; the political situation; assassination of Lincoln; end of the Confederacy; and Reconstruction.

- **Foundations of Education** includes topics such as contemporary issues in education; past and current influences on education (philosophies, democratic ideals, social/economic influences); and the interrelationships between contemporary issues and influences.

- **Life-span Developmental Psychology** covers models and theories; methods of study; ethical issues; biological development; perception, learning and memory; cognition and language; social, emotional, and personality development; social behaviors, family life cycle, extrafamilial settings; singlehood and cohabitation; occupational development and retirement; adjustment to life stresses; and bereavement and loss.

- **Drug and Alcohol Abuse** includes such topics as drug use in society; classification of drugs; pharmacological principles; alcohol (types, effects of, alcoholism); general principles and use of sedative hypnotics, narcotic analgesics, stimulants, and hallucinogens; other drugs (inhalants, steroids); and prevention/treatment.

- **General Anthropology** deals with anthropology as a discipline; theoretical perspectives; physical anthropology; archaeology; social organization; economic organization; political organization; religion; and modernization and application of anthropology.

- **Introduction to Law Enforcement** includes topics such as history and professional movement of law enforcement; overview of the U.S. criminal justice system; police systems in the U.S.; police organization, management, and issues; and U.S. law and precedents.

- **Criminal Justice** deals with criminal behavior (crime in the U.S., theories of crime, types of crime); the criminal justice system (historical origins, legal foundations, due process); police; the court system (history and organization, adult court system, juvenile court, pre-trial and post-trial processes); and corrections.

- **Fundamentals of Counseling** covers historical development (significant influences and people); counselor roles and functions; the counseling relationship; and theoretical approaches to counseling.

Business
- **Principles of Finance** deals with financial statements and planning; time value of money; working capital management; valuation and characteristics; capital budgeting; cost of capital; risk and return; and international financial management. The use of a nonprogrammable, handheld calculator is permitted.

- **Principles of Financial Accounting** includes topics such as general concepts and principles, accounting cycle and classification; transaction analysis; accruals and deferrals; cash and internal control; current accounts; long- and short-term liabilities; capital stock; and financial statements. The use of a nonprogrammable, handheld calculator is permitted.

- **Human Resource Management** covers general employment issues; job analysis; training and development; performance appraisals; compensation issues; security issues; personnel legislation and regulation; labor relations and current issues; an overview of the Human Resource Management Field; Human Resource Planning; Staffing; training and development; compensation issues; safety and health; employee rights and discipline; employment law; labor relations and current issues and trends.

- **Organizational Behavior** deals with the study of organizational behavior (scientific approaches, research designs, data collection methods); individual processes and characteristics; interpersonal and group processes and characteristics; organizational processes and characteristics; and change and development processes.

- **Principles of Supervision** deals with the roles and responsibilities of the supervisor; management functions (planning, organization and staffing, directing at the supervisory level); and other topics (legal issues, stress management, union environments, quality concerns).

- **Business Law II** covers topics such as sales of goods; debtor and creditor relations; business organizations; property; and commercial paper.

- **Introduction to Computing** includes topics such as history and technological generations; hardware/software; applications to information technology; program development; data management; communications and connectivity; and computing and society. The use of a nonprogrammable, handheld calculator is permitted.

- **Management Information Systems** covers systems theory, analysis and design of systems, hardware and software; database management; telecommunications; management of the MIS functional area and informational support.

- **Introduction to Business** deals with economic issues affecting business; international business; government and business; forms of business ownership; small business, entrepreneurship and franchise; management process; human resource management; production and operations; marketing management; financial management; risk management and insurance; and management and information systems.

- **Money and Banking** covers the role and kinds of money; commercial banks and other financial intermediaries; central banking and the Federal Reserve system; money and macroeconomics activity; monetary policy in the U.S.; and the international monetary system.

- **Personal Finance** includes topics such as financial goals and values; budgeting; credit and debt; major purchases; taxes; insurance; investments; and retirement and estate planning. The use of auxiliary materials, such as calculators and slide rules, is NOT permitted.

- **Business Mathematics** deals with basic operations with integers, fractions, and decimals; round numbers; ratios; averages; business graphs; simple interest; compound interest and annuities; net pay and deductions; discounts and markups; depreciation and net worth; corporate securities; distribution of ownership; and stock and asset turnover.

Physical Science
• **Astronomy** covers the history of astronomy, celestial mechanics; celestial systems; astronomical instruments; the solar system; nature and evolution; the galaxy; the universe; determining astronomical distances; and life in the universe.

• **Here's to Your Health** covers mental health and behavior; human development and relationships; substance abuse; fitness and nutrition; risk factors, disease, and disease prevention; and safety, consumer awareness, and environmental concerns.

• **Environment and Humanity** deals with topics such as ecological concepts (ecosystems, global ecology, food chains and webs); environmental impacts; environmental management and conservation; and political processes and the future.

• **Principles of Physical Science I** includes physics: Newton's Laws of Motion; energy and momentum; thermodynamics; wave and optics; electricity and magnetism; chemistry: properties of matter; atomic theory and structure; and chemical reactions.

• **Physical Geology** covers Earth materials; igneous, sedimentary, and metamorphic rocks; surface processes (weathering, groundwater, glaciers, oceanic systems, deserts and winds, hydrologic cycle); internal Earth processes; and applications (mineral and energy resources, environmental geology).

Applied Technology
• **Technical Writing** covers topics such as theory and practice of technical writing; purpose, content, and organizational patterns of common types of technical documents; elements of various technical reports; and technical editing. Students have the option to write a short essay on one of the technical topics provided. Thomson Prometric will not score the essay; however, for determining the award of credit, a copy of the essay will be forwarded to the college or university you've designated along with the score report or transcript.

Humanities
• **Ethics in America** deals with ethical traditions (Greek views, Biblical traditions, moral law, consequential ethics, feminist ethics); ethical analysis of issues arising in interpersonal and personal-societal relationships and in professional and occupational roles; and relationships between ethical traditions and the ethical analysis of situations. Students have the option to write an essay to analyze a morally problematic situation in terms of issues relevant to a decision and arguments for alternative positions. Thomson Prometric will not score the essay; however, for determining the award of credit, a copy of the essay will be forwarded to the college or university you've designated along with the score report or transcript.

• **Introduction to World Religions** covers topics such as dimensions and approaches to religion; primal religions; Hinduism; Buddhism; Confucianism; Taoism; Judaism; Christianity; and Islam.

• **Principles of Public Speaking** consists of two parts: Part One consists of multiple-choice questions covering considerations of Principles of Public Speaking; audience analysis; purposes of speeches; structure/organization; content/supporting materials; research; language and style; delivery; communication apprehension; listening and feedback; and criticism and evaluation. Part Two requires the student to record an impromptu persuasive speech that will be scored.

FREQUENTLY ASKED QUESTIONS ABOUT DSSTs

In order to pass the test, must I study from one of the recommended references?

The recommended references are a listing of books that were being used as textbooks in college courses of the same or similar title at the time the test was developed. Appropriate textbooks for study are not limited to those listed in the fact sheet. If you wish to obtain study resources to prepare for the examination, you may reference either the current edition of the listed titles or textbooks currently used at a local college or university for the same class title. It is recommended that you reference more than one textbook on the topics outlined in the fact sheet. You should begin by checking textbook content against the content outline included on the front page of the DSST fact sheet before selecting textbooks that cover the text content from which to study. Textbooks may be found at the campus bookstore of a local college or university offering a course on the subject.

Is there a penalty for guessing on the tests?

There is no penalty for guessing on DSSTs, so you should mark an answer for each question.

How much time will I have to complete the test?

Many DSSTs can be completed within 90 minutes; however, additional time can be allowed if necessary.

What should I do if I find a test question irregularity?

Continue testing and then report the irregularity to the test administrator after the test. This may be done by asking that the test administrator note the irregularity on the Supervisor's Irregularity Report or you can write to Thomson Prometric, DSST Program, 2000 Lenox Drive, Third Floor, Lawrenceville, NJ 08648, and indicate the form and question number(s) or circumstances as well as your name and address.

When will I receive my score report?

Allow approximately four weeks from the date of testing to receive your score report. Allow six to eight weeks to receive a score report for the *Principles of Public Speaking* examination.

Will my test scores be released without my permission?

Your test score will not be released to anyone other than the school you designate on your answer sheet unless you write to us and ask us to send a transcript elsewhere. Instructions about how to do this can be found on your score report. Your scores may be used for research purposes, but individual scores are never made public nor are individuals identified if research findings are made public.

If I do not achieve a passing score on the test, how long must I wait until I can take the test again?

If you do not receive a score on the test that will enable you to obtain credit for the course, you may take the test again after six months (180 days). Please do not attempt to take the test before six months (180 days) have passed because you will receive a score report marked <u>invalid</u> and your test fee will not be refunded.

Can my test scores be canceled?

The test administrator is required to report any irregularities to Thomson Prometric. <u>The consequence of bringing unauthorized materials into the testing room, or giving or receiving help, will be the forfeiture of your test fee and the invalidation of test scores.</u> The DSST Program reserves the right to cancel scores and not issue score reports in such situations.

What can I do if I feel that my test scores were not accurately reported?

Thomson Prometric recognizes the extreme importance of test results to candidates and has a multi-step quality-control procedure to help ensure that reported scores are accurate. If you have reason to believe that your score(s) were not accurately reported, you may request to have your answer sheet reviewed and hand scored.

The fees for this service are:
- $20 fee if requested within six months of the test date
- $30 fee if requested more than six months from the test date
- $30 fee if a re-evaluation of the *Principles of Public Speaking* speech is requested

The fee for this service can be paid by credit card or by certified check or U.S. money order payable to Thomson Prometric. Submit your request for score verification along with the appropriate fee or credit card information (credit card number and expiration date) to Thomson Prometric, DSST Program, 2000 Lenox Drive, Third Floor, Lawrenceville, NJ 08648. Include your full name, the test title, the date you took the test, and your Social Security number. Candidates will be notified if a scoring discrepancy is discovered within four weeks of receipt of the request.

What does ACE recommendation mean?

The ACE recommendation is the minimum passing score recommended by the American Council on Education for any given test. It is equivalent to the average score of students in the DSST norming sample who received a grade of C for the course. Some schools require a score higher than the ACE recommendation.

Who is NLC?

National Learning Corporation (NLC) has been successfully preparing candidates for 40 years for over 5,000 exams. NLC publishes Passbook® study guides to help candidates prepare for all DANTES and CLEP exams and almost every other type of exam from high school through adult career.

Go to our website — www.passbooks.com — or call (800) 632-8888 for information about ordering our Passbooks.

To get detailed information on the DSST program and DSST preparation materials, visit www.getcollegecredit.com.

If you are interested in taking the DSST exams, call 877-471-9860 or e-mail pnj-dsst@thomson.com.

HOW TO TAKE A TEST

You have studied long, hard and conscientiously.

With your official admission card in hand, and your heart pounding, you have been admitted to the examination room.

You note that there are several hundred other applicants in the examination room waiting to take the same test.

They all appear to be equally well prepared.

You know that nothing but your best effort will suffice. The "moment of truth" is at hand: you now have to demonstrate objectively, in writing, your knowledge of content and your understanding of subject matter.

You are fighting the most important battle of your life—to pass and/or score high on an examination which will determine your career and provide the economic basis for your livelihood.

What extra, special things should you know and should you do in taking the examination?

I. YOU MUST PASS AN EXAMINATION

A. WHAT EVERY CANDIDATE SHOULD KNOW
   Examination applicants often ask us for help in preparing for the written test. What can I study in advance? What kinds of questions will be asked? How will the test be given? How will the papers be graded?

B. HOW ARE EXAMS DEVELOPED?
   Examinations are carefully written by trained technicians who are specialists in the field known as "psychological measurement," in consultation with recognized authorities in the field of work that the test will cover. These experts recommend the subject matter areas or skills to be tested; only those knowledges or skills important to your success on the job are included. The most reliable books and source materials available are used as references. Together, the experts and technicians judge the difficulty level of the questions.
   Test technicians know how to phrase questions so that the problem is clearly stated. Their ethics do not permit "trick" or "catch" questions. Questions may have been tried out on sample groups, or subjected to statistical analysis, to determine their usefulness.
   Written tests are often used in combination with performance tests, ratings of training and experience, and oral interviews. All of these measures combine to form the best-known means of finding the right person for the right job.

II. HOW TO PASS THE WRITTEN TEST

A. BASIC STEPS

1) Study the announcement

How, then, can you know what subjects to study? Our best answer is: "Learn as much as possible about the class of positions for which you've applied." The exam will test the knowledge, skills and abilities needed to do the work.

Your most valuable source of information about the position you want is the official exam announcement. This announcement lists the training and experience qualifications. Check these standards and apply only if you come reasonably close to meeting them. Many jurisdictions preview the written test in the exam announcement by including a section called "Knowledge and Abilities Required," "Scope of the Examination," or some similar heading. Here you will find out specifically what fields will be tested.

2) Choose appropriate study materials

If the position for which you are applying is technical or advanced, you will read more advanced, specialized material. If you are already familiar with the basic principles of your field, elementary textbooks would waste your time. Concentrate on advanced textbooks and technical periodicals. Think through the concepts and review difficult problems in your field.

These are all general sources. You can get more ideas on your own initiative, following these leads. For example, training manuals and publications of the government agency which employs workers in your field can be useful, particularly for technical and professional positions. A letter or visit to the government department involved may result in more specific study suggestions, and certainly will provide you with a more definite idea of the exact nature of the position you are seeking.

3) Study this book!

III. KINDS OF TESTS

Tests are used for purposes other than measuring knowledge and ability to perform specified duties. For some positions, it is equally important to test ability to make adjustments to new situations or to profit from training. In others, basic mental abilities not dependent on information are essential. Questions which test these things may not appear as pertinent to the duties of the position as those which test for knowledge and information. Yet they are often highly important parts of a fair examination. For very general questions, it is almost impossible to help you direct your study efforts. What we can do is to point out some of the more common of these general abilities needed in public service positions and describe some typical questions.

1) General information

Broad, general information has been found useful for predicting job success in some kinds of work. This is tested in a variety of ways, from vocabulary lists to questions about current events. Basic background in some field of work, such as sociology or economics, may be sampled in a group of questions. Often these are principles which have become familiar to most persons through exposure rather than through formal training. It is difficult to advise you how to study for these questions; being alert to the world around you is our best suggestion.

2) Verbal ability

An example of an ability needed in many positions is verbal or language ability. Verbal ability is, in brief, the ability to use and understand words. Vocabulary and grammar tests are typical measures of this ability. Reading comprehension or paragraph interpretation questions are common in many kinds of civil service tests. You are given a paragraph of written material and asked to find its central meaning.

IV. KINDS OF QUESTIONS

1. Multiple-choice Questions

Most popular of the short-answer questions is the "multiple choice" or "best answer" question. It can be used, for example, to test for factual knowledge, ability to solve problems or judgment in meeting situations found at work.

A multiple-choice question is normally one of three types:
- It can begin with an incomplete statement followed by several possible endings. You are to find the one ending which best completes the statement, although some of the others may not be entirely wrong.
- It can also be a complete statement in the form of a question which is answered by choosing one of the statements listed.
- It can be in the form of a problem – again you select the best answer.

Here is an example of a multiple-choice question with a discussion which should give you some clues as to the method for choosing the right answer:

When an employee has a complaint about his assignment, the action which will best help him overcome his difficulty is to
- A. discuss his difficulty with his coworkers
- B. take the problem to the head of the organization
- C. take the problem to the person who gave him the assignment
- D. say nothing to anyone about his complaint

In answering this question, you should study each of the choices to find which is best. Consider choice "A" – Certainly an employee may discuss his complaint with fellow employees, but no change or improvement can result, and the complaint remains unresolved. Choice "B" is a poor choice since the head of the organization probably does not know what assignment you have been given, and taking your problem to him is known as "going over the head" of the supervisor. The supervisor, or person who made the assignment, is the person who can clarify it or correct any injustice. Choice "C" is, therefore, correct. To say nothing, as in choice "D," is unwise. Supervisors have and interest in knowing the problems employees are facing, and the employee is seeking a solution to his problem.

2. True/False

3. Matching Questions

Matching an answer from a column of choices within another column.

V. RECORDING YOUR ANSWERS

Computer terminals are used more and more today for many different kinds of exams.

For an examination with very few applicants, you may be told to record your answers in the test booklet itself. Separate answer sheets are much more common. If this separate answer sheet is to be scored by machine – and this is often the case – it is highly important that you mark your answers correctly in order to get credit.

VI. BEFORE THE TEST

YOUR PHYSICAL CONDITION IS IMPORTANT

If you are not well, you can't do your best work on tests. If you are half asleep, you can't do your best either. Here are some tips:

1) Get about the same amount of sleep you usually get. Don't stay up all night before the test, either partying or worrying—DON'T DO IT!
2) If you wear glasses, be sure to wear them when you go to take the test. This goes for hearing aids, too.
3) If you have any physical problems that may keep you from doing your best, be sure to tell the person giving the test. If you are sick or in poor health, you relay cannot do your best on any test. You can always come back and take the test some other time.

Common sense will help you find procedures to follow to get ready for an examination. Too many of us, however, overlook these sensible measures. Indeed, nervousness and fatigue have been found to be the most serious reasons why applicants fail to do their best on civil service tests. Here is a list of reminders:

- Begin your preparation early – Don't wait until the last minute to go scurrying around for books and materials or to find out what the position is all about.
- Prepare continuously – An hour a night for a week is better than an all-night cram session. This has been definitely established. What is more, a night a week for a month will return better dividends than crowding your study into a shorter period of time.
- Locate the place of the exam – You have been sent a notice telling you when and where to report for the examination. If the location is in a different town or otherwise unfamiliar to you, it would be well to inquire the best route and learn something about the building.
- Relax the night before the test – Allow your mind to rest. Do not study at all that night. Plan some mild recreation or diversion; then go to bed early and get a good night's sleep.
- Get up early enough to make a leisurely trip to the place for the test – This way unforeseen events, traffic snarls, unfamiliar buildings, etc. will not upset you.
- Dress comfortably – A written test is not a fashion show. You will be known by number and not by name, so wear something comfortable.
- Leave excess paraphernalia at home – Shopping bags and odd bundles will get in your way. You need bring only the items mentioned in the official notice you received; usually everything you need is provided. Do not bring reference books to the exam. They will only confuse those last minutes and be taken away from you when in the test room.

- Arrive somewhat ahead of time – If because of transportation schedules you must get there very early, bring a newspaper or magazine to take your mind off yourself while waiting.
- Locate the examination room – When you have found the proper room, you will be directed to the seat or part of the room where you will sit. Sometimes you are given a sheet of instructions to read while you are waiting. Do not fill out any forms until you are told to do so; just read them and be prepared.
- Relax and prepare to listen to the instructions
- If you have any physical problem that may keep you from doing your best, be sure to tell the test administrator. If you are sick or in poor health, you really cannot do your best on the exam. You can come back and take the test some other time.

VII. AT THE TEST

The day of the test is here and you have the test booklet in your hand. The temptation to get going is very strong. Caution! There is more to success than knowing the right answers. You must know how to identify your papers and understand variations in the type of short-answer question used in this particular examination. Follow these suggestions for maximum results from your efforts:

1) Cooperate with the monitor

The test administrator has a duty to create a situation in which you can be as much at ease as possible. He will give instructions, tell you when to begin, check to see that you are marking your answer sheet correctly, and so on. He is not there to guard you, although he will see that your competitors do not take unfair advantage. He wants to help you do your best.

2) Listen to all instructions

Don't jump the gun! Wait until you understand all directions. In most civil service tests you get more time than you need to answer the questions. So don't be in a hurry. Read each word of instructions until you clearly understand the meaning. Study the examples, listen to all announcements and follow directions. Ask questions if you do not understand what to do.

3) Identify your papers

Civil service exams are usually identified by number only. You will be assigned a number; you must not put your name on your test papers. Be sure to copy your number correctly. Since more than one exam may be given, copy your exact examination title.

4) Plan your time

Unless you are told that a test is a "speed" or "rate of work" test, speed itself is usually not important. Time enough to answer all the questions will be provided, but this does not mean that you have all day. An overall time limit has been set. Divide the total time (in minutes) by the number of questions to determine the approximate time you have for each question.

5) Do not linger over difficult questions

If you come across a difficult question, mark it with a paper clip (useful to have along) and come back to it when you have been through the booklet. One caution if you do this – be sure to skip a number on your answer sheet as well. Check often to be sure that you have not lost your place and that you are marking in the row numbered the same as the question you are answering.

6) Read the questions

Be sure you know what the question asks! Many capable people are unsuccessful because they failed to read the questions correctly.

7) Answer all questions

Unless you have been instructed that a penalty will be deducted for incorrect answers, it is better to guess than to omit a question.

8) Speed tests

It is often better NOT to guess on speed tests. It has been found that on timed tests people are tempted to spend the last few seconds before time is called in marking answers at random – without even reading them – in the hope of picking up a few extra points. To discourage this practice, the instructions may warn you that your score will be "corrected" for guessing. That is, a penalty will be applied. The incorrect answers will be deducted from the correct ones, or some other penalty formula will be used.

9) Review your answers

If you finish before time is called, go back to the questions you guessed or omitted to give them further thought. Review other answers if you have time.

10) Return your test materials

If you are ready to leave before others have finished or time is called, take ALL your materials to the monitor and leave quietly. Never take any test material with you. The monitor can discover whose papers are not complete, and taking a test booklet may be grounds for disqualification.

VIII. EXAMINATION TECHNIQUES

1) Read the general instructions carefully. These are usually printed on the first page of the exam booklet. As a rule, these instructions refer to the timing of the examination; the fact that you should not start work until the signal and must stop work at a signal, etc. If there are any special instructions, such as a choice of questions to be answered, make sure that you note this instruction carefully.

2) When you are ready to start work on the examination, that is as soon as the signal has been given, read the instructions to each question booklet, underline any key words or phrases, such as least, best, outline, describe and the like. In this way you will tend to answer as requested rather than discover on reviewing your paper that you listed without describing, that you selected the worst choice rather than the best choice, etc.

3) If the examination is of the objective or multiple-choice type – that is, each question will also give a series of possible answers: A, B, C or D, and you are called upon to select the best answer and write the letter next to that answer on your answer paper – it is advisable to start answering each question in turn. There may be anywhere from 50 to 100 such questions in the three or four hours allotted and you can see how much time would be taken if you read through all the questions before beginning to answer any. Furthermore, if you

come across a question or group of questions which you know would be difficult to answer, it would undoubtedly affect your handling of all the other questions.

4) If the examination is of the essay type and contains but a few questions, it is a moot point as to whether you should read all the questions before starting to answer any one. Of course, if you are given a choice – say five out of seven and the like – then it is essential to read all the questions so you can eliminate the two that are most difficult. If, however, you are asked to answer all the questions, there may be danger in trying to answer the easiest one first because you may find that you will spend too much time on it. The best technique is to answer the first question, then proceed to the second, etc.

5) Time your answers. Before the exam begins, write down the time it started, then add the time allowed for the examination and write down the time it must be completed, then divide the time available somewhat as follows:
   - If 3-1/2 hours are allowed, that would be 210 minutes. If you have 80 objective-type questions, that would be an average of 2-1/2 minutes per question. Allow yourself no more than 2 minutes per question, or a total of 160 minutes, which will permit about 50 minutes to review.
   - If for the time allotment of 210 minutes there are 7 essay questions to answer, that would average about 30 minutes a question. Give yourself only 25 minutes per question so that you have about 35 minutes to review.

6) The most important instruction is to read each question and make sure you know what is wanted. The second most important instruction is to time yourself properly so that you answer every question. The third most important instruction is to answer every question. Guess if you have to but include something for each question. Remember that you will receive no credit for a blank and will probably receive some credit if you write something in answer to an essay question. If you guess a letter – say "B" for a multiple-choice question – you may have guessed right. If you leave a blank as an answer to a multiple-choice question, the examiners may respect your feelings but it will not add a point to your score. Some exams may penalize you for wrong answers, so in such cases only, you may not want to guess unless you have some basis for your answer.

7) Suggestions
   a. Objective-type questions
      1. Examine the question booklet for proper sequence of pages and questions
      2. Read all instructions carefully
      3. Skip any question which seems too difficult; return to it after all other questions have been answered
      4. Apportion your time properly; do not spend too much time on any single question or group of questions
      5. Note and underline key words – all, most, fewest, least, best, worst, same, opposite, etc.
      6. Pay particular attention to negatives
      7. Note unusual option, e.g., unduly long, short, complex, different or similar in content to the body of the question
      8. Observe the use of "hedging" words – probably, may, most likely, etc.

9. Make sure that your answer is put next to the same number as the question
10. Do not second-guess unless you have good reason to believe the second answer is definitely more correct
11. Cross out original answer if you decide another answer is more accurate; do not erase until you are ready to hand your paper in
12. Answer all questions; guess unless instructed otherwise
13. Leave time for review

b. Essay questions
1. Read each question carefully
2. Determine exactly what is wanted. Underline key words or phrases.
3. Decide on outline or paragraph answer
4. Include many different points and elements unless asked to develop any one or two points or elements
5. Show impartiality by giving pros and cons unless directed to select one side only
6. Make and write down any assumptions you find necessary to answer the questions
7. Watch your English, grammar, punctuation and choice of words
8. Time your answers; don't crowd material

8) Answering the essay question

Most essay questions can be answered by framing the specific response around several key words or ideas. Here are a few such key words or ideas:

M's: manpower, materials, methods, money, management
P's: purpose, program, policy, plan, procedure, practice, problems, pitfalls, personnel, public relations

a. Six basic steps in handling problems:
1. Preliminary plan and background development
2. Collect information, data and facts
3. Analyze and interpret information, data and facts
4. Analyze and develop solutions as well as make recommendations
5. Prepare report and sell recommendations
6. Install recommendations and follow up effectiveness

b. Pitfalls to avoid
1. Taking things for granted – A statement of the situation does not necessarily imply that each of the elements is necessarily true; for example, a complaint may be invalid and biased so that all that can be taken for granted is that a complaint has been registered
2. Considering only one side of a situation – Wherever possible, indicate several alternatives and then point out the reasons you selected the best one
3. Failing to indicate follow up – Whenever your answer indicates action on your part, make certain that you will take proper follow-up action to see how successful your recommendations, procedures or actions turn out to be
4. Taking too long in answering any single question – Remember to time your answers properly

EXAMINATION SECTION

EXAMINATION SECTION
TEST 1

DIRECTIONS: Each question or incomplete statement is followed by several suggested answers or completions. Select the one that BEST answers the question or completes the statement. *PRINT THE LETTER OF THE CORRECT ANSWER IN THE SPACE AT THE RIGHT.*

1. A crime that has no purpose except to accomplish the behavior at hand, rather than for monetary gain, is described as 1.____

    A. mercenary
    B. expressive
    C. random
    D. instrumental

2. A _____ perspective on crime maintains that crime rates are a function of neighborhood characteristics and cultural forces. 2.____

    A. conflict   B. structural   C. choice   D. process

3. Of the following crimes, which is most likely to occur in a public place rather than in the home? 3.____

    A. Robbery   B. Rape   C. Murder   D. Assault

4. The first correctional reforms in the United States began at the end of the 17th century in the state of 4.____

    A. Kentucky
    B. Pennsylvania
    C. New York
    D. Massachusetts

5. An act or conduct that is declared by statute to be an offense, but only when committed or engaged in by a juvenile, and that can only be adjudicated by a juvenile court, is known as a 5.____

    A. misdemeanor
    B. delinquent act
    C. malfeasance
    D. status offense

6. Most large prisons are divided into the two major operating units of 6.____

    A. planning and procedure
    B. custody and treatment
    C. correction and maintenance
    D. administration and operations

7. Which of the following is a type of labeling theory concerning crime? 7.____

    A. Focal concern theory
    B. Containment theory
    C. Neutralization theory
    D. The general theory of deviance

8. Which of the following is NOT typically a role played by a prosecutor in a criminal justice system? 8.____

    A. Determining charges
    B. Representing the government at appeals
    C. Determining the conditions under which probation may be revoked
    D. Conducting investigations of law violations

9. The self-report study for measuring crime usually focuses on

   A. juvenile delinquencies and youth crimes
   B. public order crimes
   C. violent crimes
   D. substance abuse crimes

10. The highest level of most state courts consists of the

    A. trial courts
    B. appellate courts
    C. magistrates
    D. courts of special jurisdiction

11. Between 1983 and 1993 in the United States, violent crime

    A. decreased slightly, by a few percentage points
    B. stayed at about the same rate
    C. increased by about 10 percent
    D. increased by about 40 percent

12. Probably the most common criminal offense is

    A. larceny/theft
    B. substance abuse
    C. computer crime
    D. prostitution

13. Which of the following bail alternatives is a form of nonfinancial release?

    A. Release on recognizance
    B. Unsecured bail
    C. Property bail
    D. Surety bail

14. In which of the following court cases was it ruled that an indigent defendant subjected to a felony prosecution must have counsel provided by the state?

    A. Mapp v. Ohio (1961)
    B. Gideon v. Wainwright (1963)
    C. Rhodes v. Chapman (1981)
    D. Arizona v. Hicks (1987)

15. A diagnosis or classification center is a functional unit within a

    A. criminal court that determines in which order the cases in its caseload will be heard
    B. prosecutor's office that determines which crime or crimes a person in custody will be charged with
    C. correctional institution that holds a person held in custody for the purpose of determining to which correctional facility or program they should be committed
    D. correctional institution that is used for the treatment of persons held in custody who are mentally or physically ill

16. What is the term for the determination of guilt or innocence concerning criminal charges?

    A. Jurisdiction
    B. Verdict
    C. Review
    D. Adjudication

17. Which of the following is a type of choice theory concerning crime?

   A. Routine activities
   B. Containment
   C. Cognitive
   D. General strain

18. To most people, the best way to distinguish immoral acts from crimes is to focus on the issue of

   A. feelings of remorse
   B. motivation
   C. harm to society
   D. intent

19. Each of the following is a commonly voiced concern with the FBI's Uniform Crime Report (UCR) as a measurement of criminal offenses in the United States EXCEPT

   A. the way different police departments record and report criminal activity varies widely
   B. reports are compulsory and may not be enthusiastically researched or submitted
   C. many serious crimes are not reported by victims to police
   D. federal crimes are not included

20. Approximately what percentage of the United States prison population is white?

   A. 10   B. 20   C. 35   D. 55

21. The _____ view or crime, which holds that crimes are behaviors that are considered to be repugnant to all elements of society, dominated American criminology until the late 1960s.

   A. progressive
   B. conflict
   C. consensus
   D. interactional

22. In which of the following court cases was it ruled that an effort must be made in open court to question the defendant on the voluntariness of an admission of guilt before a guilty plea can be accepted?

   A. Boykin v. Alabama
   B. Brady v. United States
   C. Bordenkircher v. Hayes
   D. Santobello v. New York

23. Which of the following is/are an example of collateral business crime?

   A. Antitrust violations
   B. Fraudulent land sales
   C. Bribery
   D. Welfare fraud

24. An offender is sentenced to a maximum prison term for an offense. After being incarcerated for approximately 90 days, the offender is then resentenced to probation. In this case, the court has implemented a form of correction known as

   A. split sentencing
   B. shock incarceration
   C. intensive probation supervision
   D. shock probation

25. Approximately what percentage of all reported index crimes are cleared by arrest?

   A. 10   B. 20   C. 40   D. 60

KEY (CORRECT ANSWERS)

1.	B	11.	D
2.	B	12.	A
3.	A	13.	A
4.	B	14.	B
5.	D	15.	C
6.	B	16.	D
7.	D	17.	A
8.	C	18.	C
9.	A	19.	B
10.	B	20.	C

21. C
22. A
23. A
24. D
25. B

TEST 2

DIRECTIONS: Each question or incomplete statement is followed by several suggested answers or completions. Select the one that BEST answers the question or completes the statement. *PRINT THE LETTER OF THE CORRECT ANSWER IN THE SPACE AT THE RIGHT.*

1. The major premise of the social development theory of crime is that   1.____

    A. crime and criminality are separate concepts; people choose to commit crime when they lack self-control
    B. weak social controls produce crime
    C. people choose to commit crime when they are biologically and psychologically impaired
    D. delinquency is a function of family life, which is controlled by the economic system

2. The crime control model of criminal justice emphasizes   2.____

    A. state-supported social control
    B. the rehabilitation of criminals
    C. nonintervention
    D. the protection of society and compensation of victims

3. The Auburn and Pennsylvania prison systems in the United States were examples of prisons designed specifically for the purpose of   3.____

    A. deterrence   B. retribution
    C. incapacitation   D. rehabilitation

4. According to social learning theorists, there are four factors that help to produce violence and aggression.   4.____
Which of the following is NOT one of these?

    A. An inherent tendency to act violently
    B. Learned aggressive responses
    C. An event that heightens arousal
    D. The belief that aggression will be rewarded

5. The American judicial system is characterized by each of the following EXCEPT   5.____

    A. specialization
    B. organization according to case typology
    C. an absence of supervisory control
    D. a dual system of courts

6. The view that the violent prison subculture reflects the criminal culture of the outside world, and is neither developed in or unique to prisons, is the _____ model.   6.____

    A. importation   B. developmental
    C. interactional   D. institutional

7. Which of the following occurs earliest in the criminal justice process?   7.____

    A. Custody   B. Preliminary hearing
    C. Arraignment   D. Charging

8. Supporters of the plea bargaining process in the American criminal justice system frequently argue each of the following EXCEPT
   A. it improves the administrative efficiency of the courts
   B. the defendant is able to avoid possible detention and extended trial and may receive a reduced sentence
   C. it tends to even out the disparities in sentencing that are common in the justice system
   D. it reduces the overall financial cost of criminal prosecution

9. In what year were juvenile offenders in the United States granted the right to counsel?
   A. 1868   B. 1932   C. 1954   D. 1968

10. Which of the following is a biosocial theory of crime?
    A. Cognitive   B. Behavioral
    C. Psychodynamic   D. Neurological

11. Which of the following has generally proven to be most successful as a means of correction in the United States?
    A. Split sentencing   B. Restitution
    C. Residential community centers   D. Incarceration

12. The fact-finding process wherein a juvenile court determines whether there is sufficient evidence to sustain the allegations in a petition is known as a(n) _____ hearing.
    A. indictment   B. detention
    C. adjudicatory   D. disposition

13. Which of the following is NOT within the jurisdiction of a federal magistrate's court?
    A. Reviewing and enforcing actions/orders of other agencies or departments
    B. Setting bond
    C. Trying misdemeanors
    D. Issuing warrants

14. Most involuntary manslaughter cases involve
    A. street/bar fights   B. domestic disputes
    C. workplace crimes   D. motor vehicle deaths

15. It is generally agreed that the first modern jail in the United States was
    A. Castle Island in Massachusetts
    B. Walnut Street Prison in Pennsylvania
    C. Elmira Reformatory in New York
    D. Auburn Prison in New York

16. The principle of giving jailed inmates the minimum comforts required by law, in order to contain the costs of incarceration, is
    A. caveat emptor   B. constabular sanctions
    C. custodial convenience   D. relative deprivation

17. Each of the following is a way in which female prison life generally differs from that in male institutions in the United States EXCEPT

    A. female inmates do not form cohesive groups
    B. they do not operate according to a rigid, anti-authority social code
    C. they are more often controlled with mood-altering drugs than males
    D. they are more likely to project their anger inward and revert to self-destructive behavior

18. The broad category of public order crimes are also sometimes referred to as _____ crimes.

    A. victimless   B. collateral
    C. violent   D. mala prohibitum

19. According to the FBI's Unified Crime Report (UCR), which of the following is a Part II offense?

    A. Auto theft   B. Aggravated assault
    C. Counterfeiting   D. Arson

20. In 1931, President Herbert Hoover appointed the _____ Commission, a national study group which analyzed the American criminal justice system and helped usher in the era of treatment and rehabilitation in the United States correctional system.

    A. Chicago Crime
    B. Wickersham
    C. Cleveland Crime
    D. Law Enforcement Assistance

21. At an arraignment hearing, a judge will typically do each of the following EXCEPT

    A. inform the defendant of the sentence that will be received upon conviction
    B. ensure that the accused is properly represented by counsel
    C. inform the defendant of the charge
    D. determine whether the accused should be released on bail or some alternative plan pending a hearing or trial

22. Which element of the United States criminal justice system constitutes the greatest number of agencies?

    A. The courts   B. Police
    C. Federal law enforcement   D. Corrections

23. In ancient Rome, the only crime for which capital punishment could be officially implemented was

    A. stealing   B. murder   C. rape   D. extortion

24. An order of a superior court requesting that the record of an inferior court (or administrative body) be brought forward for review or inspection is called a writ of

    A. execution   B. habeas corpus
    C. certiorari   D. mandamus

25. Antisocial careers are often created in a series of stages. The process typically begins with 25.___

    A. violent performances
    B. the brutalization process
    C. virulency
    D. a psychotic break

KEY (CORRECT ANSWERS)

1. B
2. D
3. D
4. A
5. B

6. A
7. A
8. C
9. D
10. D

11. B
12. C
13. A
14. D
15. B

16. C
17. A
18. A
19. C
20. B

21. A
22. A
23. A
24. C
25. B

EXAMINATION SECTION
TEST 1

DIRECTIONS: Each question or incomplete statement is followed by several suggested answers or completions. Select the one that BEST answers the question or completes the statement. *PRINT THE LETTER OF THE CORRECT ANSWER IN THE SPACE AT THE RIGHT.*

1. The value orientations of lower-class cultures include the need for trouble, excitement, smartness, fate, and personal autonomy. These value orientations are known as

    A. degenerate anomalies
    B. focal concerns
    C. niches
    D. folkways

    1.____

2. Currently, about 16 states have adopted what is known as the Missouri Plan for selecting state court judges. Which of the following is an element of the Missouri Plan?

    A. The state senate makes appointments from a list provided by the state assembly.
    B. An elected official makes appointments from a list provided by a nominating commission.
    C. Candidates are assigned strictly by merit, measured on a quantified and scaled set of criteria.
    D. Partisan elections after two candidates have been chosen for a seat on the bench.

    2.____

3. The PRIMARY reason for developing alternative sanctions in the American corrections system has been the need

    A. to develop punishments that are fair and proportional
    B. to raise revenue generated through fines and forfeiture
    C. to develop alternatives to prisons
    D. for more punitive forms of correction

    3.____

4. In the last 25 years or so, public support of _____ has tended to increase more than the support of other factors associated with limiting crime.

    A. rehabilitation
    B. deterrence
    C. alternative sanctions
    D. probation

    4.____

5. Approximately what percentage of United States criminal justice agencies are part of local governmental structures?

    A. 25   B. 40   C. 65   D. 80

    5.____

6. Which of the following statements about the demographics of American jail inmates over the past decade is TRUE?
The

    A. percentage of Hispanic inmates has increased more than that of African-Americans
    B. number of inmates of all racial and ethnic groups has increased at the same rate
    C. percentage of white jail inmates has remained stable, while the percentage of African-American inmates has increased dramatically
    D. majority of jail inmates are poor whites

    6.____

7. What is the term for the winning party in a lower court who argues on appeal that the lower court's decision was correctly made?

   A. Appellant
   B. Respondent
   C. Appellee
   D. Plaintiff

8. The reason why many juvenile courts are empowered to act in ways that are inconsistent with the procedural safeguards available to adults in the regular courts is that

   A. juveniles are considered to have few rights
   B. the higher volume of juvenile cases requires more expedient procedures
   C. the ostensible purpose of the court is to treat and help rather than judge guilt or innocence
   D. the adversarial system is considered to be poor role modeling for young citizens

9. United States law enforcement agencies can trace their origins most closely to those in

   A. 17th century central Europe
   B. ancient China
   C. 19th century England
   D. ancient Rome

10. The nation's first formal police department was created in the city of _____ in the year 1838.

    A. Boston
    B. Baltimore
    C. New York
    D. Philadelphia

11. A charge of _____ indicates the unlawful entry of a structure, with or without force, with intent to commit a felony or larceny.

    A. breaking and entering
    B. grand larceny
    C. robbery
    D. burglary

12. In the 1960s, the first area of change in the reform of United States prisons involved

    A. medical rights
    B. freedom of the press and speech
    C. cruel and unusual punishment
    D. freedom of religion

13. In 1868, the _____ Amendment to the Constitution made the first ten amendments (the Bill of Rights) binding on the state governments.

    A. Tenth
    B. Twelfth
    C. Fourteenth
    D. Sixteenth

14. The first true juvenile court in the United States was formed in

    A. Virginia, in 1658
    B. Boston, in 1784
    C. Chicago, in 1899
    D. New York, in 1966

15. Which of the following is a form of the social disorganization theory of crime?

    A. General strain theory
    B. Concentric zone theory
    C. Relative deprivation
    D. Anomie theory

16. What is the term for a formal accusation made by a grand jury upon their own motion, either upon their own evidence or upon evidence before them?

    A. Information
    B. Presentment
    C. Complaint
    D. Indictment

17. What is the term for the group of punishments for criminal offenders that falls between probation and prison?

    A. Constables
    B. Status offense sanctions
    C. Alternative sanctions
    D. Adjudicatory penalties

18. In prisons, the method of milieu therapy is sometimes used to treat inmates. The main point of this method is to

    A. use the social structure and processes of the institution to influence the behavior patterns of inmates
    B. use specific rewards for behavior to develop positive traits
    C. encourage inmates to identify the different aspects of their own personalities and to be their own therapists
    D. help satisfy inmates' needs to feel worthwhile to themselves and others

19. Each of the following is a personality trait associated with latent delinquency in juvenile offenders EXCEPT

    A. satisfying instinctive urges without consideration of right and wrong
    B. considering satisfaction of personal needs more important than relating to others
    C. a complete absence of any outward displays of emotion
    D. the need to seek immediate gratification

20. The Salient Factor Score Index is a device that is used

    A. in criminal courts to determine the sentence for specific crimes
    B. in prisons to determine which treatment unit of a correctional institution will handle a new inmate
    C. to measure the incidence of certain types of crime in the United States
    D. in parole hearings to predict whether a candidate will be able to successfully negotiate the terms of parole

21. The Uniform Crime Reports (UCR) denotes *crime rate* as the number of offenses recorded per _____ population.

    A. 1,000   B. 10,000   C. 100,000   D. 1,000,000

22. In today's local police forces, the most significant consequences of the police subculture include a(n)

    I. mistrust of the public they serve
    II. ever-narrowing range of cases in which *personal discretion,* rather than strict policy, may be applied
    III. resistance to change

    The CORRECT answer is:

    A. I *only*   B. II *only*   C. I, III   D. II, III

23. Terrorists and other agents of political violence are sometimes referred to collectively as _____ criminals.

    A. expressive
    B. convictional
    C. revolutionary
    D. instrumental

24. For many years, United States courts did not interfere in the operation of prisons, maintaining what is called the *hands-off doctrine*. The hands-off doctrine was based on each of the following situations or beliefs EXCEPT the

    A. society's general apathy toward the prison
    B. belief that prisoners' complaints involved privileges rather than rights
    C. belief that punishment and incapacitation were the sole purpose of incarceration
    D. judiciary's belief that it lacked technical competence in prison administration

25. Which of the following terms does NOT mean the same as the others?

    A. Petit jury
    B. Jury
    C. Grand jury
    D. Trial jury

KEY (CORRECT ANSWERS)

1.	B	11.	D
2.	B	12.	D
3.	C	13.	C
4.	B	14.	C
5.	D	15.	B
6.	C	16.	B
7.	C	17.	C
8.	C	18.	A
9.	C	19.	C
10.	A	20.	D

21. C
22. C
23. B
24. C
25. C

TEST 2

DIRECTIONS: Each question or incomplete statement is followed by several suggested answers or completions. Select the one that BEST answers the question or completes the statement. *PRINT THE LETTER OF THE CORRECT ANSWER IN THE SPACE AT THE RIGHT.*

1. Which of the following is NOT a major role of most state police? 1.____

    A. Helping to trace stolen automobiles
    B. Controlling traffic on the highway system
    C. Investigating crimes
    D. Aiding in disturbances and crowd control

2. Which of the following theories of crime holds that the criminal justice system is an agent of class warfare? 2.____

    A. Instrumentalism
    B. Left realism
    C. Differential social control
    D. Marxism

3. In colonial America, the most important law enforcement agent was usually the 3.____

    A. county sheriff
    B. town marshal
    C. constable
    D. justice of the peace

4. In the court case Miranda v. Arizona (1966), it was ruled that 4.____

    A. a judge may issue a search warrant based on the *totality of the circumstances* of the case
    B. the police have a duty to warn a suspect in custody of the basic Fifth Amendment right against self incrimination
    C. the police do not need a warrant to search trash left at the curbside
    D. a dangerous person may be held in pretrial detention without bail

5. In the United States, criticism of most justice of the peace courts tends to focus on 5.____

    A. a frequent focus on social services rather than administering the law
    B. the lack of legal training required to become a justice of the peace
    C. a failure to firmly direct court proceedings
    D. the narrow role assumed by the courts

6. The illegal dumping of toxic wastes is most accurately described as a(n) _____ crime. 6.____

    A. index
    B. strict-liability
    C. negligent
    D. mala prohibitum

7. Research on the general deterrence of noncapital crimes is difficult for each of the following reasons EXCEPT the 7.____

    A. difficulty in isolating the variables for examination, such as certainty of punishment, from other factors that may affect crime rates, such as poverty
    B. inability to positively state that a correlation indicates a cause/effect relationship
    C. difficulty in making a punishment suit a particular crime
    D. difficulty in accurately measuring crimes and punishments

8. A criminal defendant's due process rights are guaranteed by the _____ Amendments to the Constitution.

   A. Fourth and Fifth
   B. Fifth and Sixth
   C. Fifth and Fourteenth
   D. Twelfth and Fourteenth

9. In a typical criminal trial, a judge's instructions to the jury on the law, evidence, and standards of proof are delivered just

   A. before the prosecutor's opening statement to the jury
   B. after the defense attorney's opening statement to the jury
   C. after the defense attorney's cross-examination
   D. after the prosecutor's closing statements

10. Which of the following statements does NOT accurately describe crime trends in the United States?

    A. Areas with low per capita crime rates tend to be rural.
    B. The western states have the highest crime and violence rates.
    C. Most reported crimes occur in the cold winter months of January and February.
    D. Firearms are involved in nearly 70 percent of all homicides.

11. Which of the following is a common criticism that is leveled against the policy of community policing?

    A. Community relations degraded through frequent contact with officers
    B. An officially unrealistic definition of what comprises a *community*
    C. A generalized deterioration of the image of the local police
    D. Increased levels of a community's fear of crime

12. The formal written accusation, filed in a court, alleging that a specified person has committed a specified offense, is known as a

    A. charging document
    B. summons
    C. complaint
    D. citation

13. While private industry programs in United States prisons have proven to be effective at teaching skills to inmates in desirable commercial areas, they have been considered to be less useful than other treatment programs because

    A. this type of education is considered to be too limiting
    B. such programs have so far been able to use only a small percentage of available inmates
    C. such programs are believed to fuel mercenary interests
    D. on the outside, most jobs in these areas also require some type of advanced educational degree

14. The most commonly used correctional method used in the United States today is

    A. incapacitation
    B. probation
    C. treatment
    D. incarceration

15. Over time, the classical theory of crime has evolved into a set of beliefs known as _____ theory.

    A. structural
    B. integrated
    C. choice
    D. conflict

16. Which of the following federal laws established a determinate sentencing system for drug crimes?

    A. 1984 Crime Control Act
    B. 1986 Anti-Drug Abuse Act
    C. 1988 Anti-Drug Abuse Act
    D. Crime Control Act of 1990

17. Which of the following is a component belief of the justice model of criminal justice?

    A. It is futile to rehabilitate criminals, because treatment programs are ineffective.
    B. The more the government intervenes in the lives of people, the greater the harm done to their future behavior patterns.
    C. Given the proper care and treatment, criminals can be changed into productive, law-abiding citizens.
    D. The justice system is a state-initiated and state-supported effort to control society.

18. In a criminal trial, a motion for a directed verdict is made by a

    A. prosecutor when the case against a defendant is so overwhelmingly convincing that a jury consultation would be a waste of the court's resources
    B. prosecutor whenever a defendant appears before court at the onset of a trial for an index crime
    C. defender when the prosecution has failed to make an adequate case against the defendant
    D. defender when the accused intends to throw himself or herself at the mercy of the court

19. What is the term for a court decision that postpones the setting of a penalty for a crime?

    A. Suspended imposition
    B. Suspended execution
    C. Indeterminate sentence
    D. Suspended sentence

20. Currently, the practice of plea bargaining occurs in about _____ percent of all criminal trials.

    A. 15
    B. 45
    C. 75
    D. 90

21. It is stated specifically in the Bill of Rights that police must follow certain guidelines in the searching for and seizing evidence. This is the basis for the

    A. Civil Rights Act of 1964
    B. exclusionary rule
    C. concept of substantive due process
    D. blue laws

22. Which of the following alternative sanctions is generally considered to be least severe?

    A. Intensive probation
    B. Split sentencing
    C. Forfeiture
    D. House arrest

23. The process in which crime rate declines with a perpetrator's age is known as

    A. disposition B. desistance
    C. diversion D. disputation

24. Which of the following crimes is unique in its requirement of victim dissent?

    A. Robbery B. Rape C. Assault D. Larceny

25. Crime Index offenses, or index crimes, is a UCR classification that includes all Part I offenses with the exception of

    A. auto theft B. arson
    C. involuntary manslaughter D. criminal homicide

KEY (CORRECT ANSWERS)

1.	C	11.	B
2.	D	12.	C
3.	A	13.	B
4.	B	14.	B
5.	B	15.	C
6.	B	16.	A
7.	C	17.	A
8.	C	18.	C
9.	D	19.	A
10.	C	20.	D

21. B
22. C
23. B
24. B
25. C

EXAMINATION SECTION
TEST 1

DIRECTIONS: Each question or incomplete statement is followed by several suggested answers or completions. Select the one that BEST answers the question or completes the statement. *PRINT THE LETTER OF THE CORRECT ANSWER IN THE SPACE AT THE RIGHT.*

1. In which of the following situations would local police NOT be justified in conducting a search without a search warrant?

    A. Seizure of nonphysical evidence, such as an overheard conversation
    B. An automobile is searched because it is believed to have been involved in a crime
    C. A search of a person is made incident to a lawful arrest
    D. A search of a private residence if a suspected criminal is seen fleeing into the residence

    1.____

2. Which of the following is NOT generally viewed as a purpose of community-based corrections?
    To

    A. protect first-time or nonserious offenders from the stigma and pain of imprisonment
    B. reduce the expense of supervising inmates
    C. increase the scrutiny to which an inmate's rehabilitation process is subjected
    D. protect the prisons system from an overwhelming influx of prisoners

    2.____

3. Under a typical prison administrative structure, the function of keeping inmate records is usually performed by the department led by the

    A. associate warden for classification and treatment
    B. associate warden for custody
    C. business manager
    D. medical services manager

    3.____

4. Under prescribed conditions, and for certain types of offenses, law enforcement officers may issue citations in lieu of arrest. A citation in lieu of arrest is warranted in each of the following situations EXCEPT

    A. the accused is identified as a member of the local community
    B. it is not yet determinable where the accused will appear to answer charges
    C. the offense is a misdemeanor where there is no danger of physical harm
    D. there is no reason to believe that the accused will flee from the jurisdiction

    4.____

5. Although there is no set standard for how *speedy* a criminal defendant's trial must be, the Federal Speedy Trial Act of 1970 mandates _____ days from arrest to indictment, and _____ days from indictment to trial.

    A. 10; 30   B. 15; 45   C. 30; 70   D. 60; 120

    5.____

6. In the nineteenth century, some prisons used the _____ system, in which officials sold the labor of inmates to private businesses.

    A. convict-lease   B. state account
    C. contract   D. Auburn

    6.____

7. Acts that are outlawed because they violate basic moral values, such as rape, murder, assault, and robbery, are known as _____ crimes.

   A. mala in se
   B. hate
   C. mala prohibitum
   D. instrumental

8. Which of the following statements is NOT an accurate description of the general demographics of crime in the United States?

   A. The effect of income has little influence on black crime rates.
   B. Poor whites are more violent than affluent whites.
   C. Most crimes are committed by people aged 18-25.
   D. Lower-class juvenile girls are more criminal than upper-class girls.

9. When a jail term is made a condition of probation, the court has implemented a form of correction known as

   A. split sentencing
   B. shock probation
   C. intensive probation
   D. shock incarceration

10. United States court rulings have provided each of the following as a federally mandated guideline for local police in their application of the Miranda rule EXCEPT

    A. people who are mentally ill due to clinically diagnosed schizophrenia may voluntarily confess and waive their Miranda rights
    B. suspects must be aware of all the possible outcomes of waiving their rights in order for the Miranda warning to be considered properly given
    C. evidence that is obtained in violation of the Miranda rule may be used by the government to impeach a defendant's testimony during trial
    D. the erroneous admission of a coerced confession at trial can be ruled a *harmless error* that would not automatically result in overturning a conviction

11. In the criminal justice system, what is the term for the set of facts and circumstances that would induce a reasonably intelligent and prudent person to believe that an accused person had committed a specific crime?

    A. Reasonable doubt
    B. Probable cause
    C. Warranted suspicion
    D. Burden of proof

12. In the court case Procunier v. Martinez, it was ruled that

    A. a prison inmate had the right to have adequate medical care
    B. an inmate's mail could be censored only if there existed substantial belief that its contents would threaten security
    C. the right of an inmate to grant press interviews could be limited
    D. the practice of double-bunking inmates in a small cell was not unconstitutional

13. Which of the following statements about murder in the United States is FALSE?

    A. Most victims know or are acquainted with their assailant.
    B. Most murders involve firearms.
    C. Most murders occur during the commission of a felony.
    D. Murder rates are highest in the South and West.

14. In most United States communities, the primary function of the local police can best be described as

    A. peace-keeping, dispute-settling agents of public health and safety
    B. symbols of public morality and stability
    C. investigators of crime and enforcers of the rule of law
    D. providers of emergency services

15. Most prison inmates in the United States are serving time for

    A. drug trafficking   B. burglary
    C. robbery   D. larceny

16. In general, the personality of members of the law enforcement community is characterized by each of the following EXCEPT

    A. insecurity   B. individualism
    C. conservatism   D. secrecy

17. Reducing burglaries in a housing project by increasing lighting and installing security alarms is an example of

    A. absolute deterrence   B. diffusion of benefits
    C. discouragement   D. situational crime prevention

18. Each of the following is considered to be a pre-trial process EXCEPT

    A. booking   B. detention
    C. arraignment   D. grand jury examination

19. The Differential _____ Theory explains criminal behavior by postulating that when people consider the available legitimate and illegitimate behaviors, they select the alternative that is perceived to be the best.

    A. Identification   B. Association Reinforcement
    C. Anticipation   D. Association

20. Any *offensive touching* is known in criminal terms as

    A. abuse   B. battery   C. rape   D. assault

21. The modern American police department was born out of urban mob violence that occurred in the United States during the _____ century.

    A. late seventeenth   B. late eighteenth
    C. early nineteenth   D. early twentieth

22. Each of the following is a system that has been developed in the American criminal justice system for providing legal counsel to the indigent EXCEPT

    A. assigning private attorneys on a case-by-case basis
    B. creating a publicly funded defender's office
    C. assigning attorneys from other courts—juvenile, probate, or district courts—on a rotating basis
    D. contracting with a law firm or group of private attorneys to regularly provide services

23. What is the term for the revocation of a person's probationary status for violation of probation rules?

    A. Alternative sanction
    B. Technical violation
    C. Status offense
    D. Determinate sentencing

24. According to most surveys and research, approximately what percentage of their working hours do most local police devote to crime-related activity?

    A. 1-5   B. 10-25   C. 40-60   D. 55-75

25. Which of the following choice theories of crime best shows the relationship between crime and punishment?

    A. Specific deterrence
    B. Rational choice
    C. Incapacitation
    D. General deterrence

KEY (CORRECT ANSWERS)

1. D		11. B	
2. C		12. B	
3. A		13. C	
4. B		14. A	
5. C		15. C	
6. C		16. B	
7. A		17. D	
8. D		18. C	
9. A		19. C	
10. B		20. B	

21. C
22. C
23. B
24. B
25. D

TEST 2

DIRECTIONS: Each question or incomplete statement is followed by several suggested answers or completions. Select the one that BEST answers the question or completes the statement. *PRINT THE LETTER OF THE CORRECT ANSWER IN THE SPACE AT THE RIGHT.*

1. Approximately what percentage of the United States correctional population is on probation?

   A. 10   B. 30   C. 65   D. 80

2. A criminal case that is tried afresh, as if there had been no earlier decision in a lower court, is said to be tried

   A. cum laude
   B. a priori
   C. de novo
   D. pro bono

3. Which of the following is a crime-specific policing strategy?

   A. Problem-oriented policing
   B. Crackdown
   C. Team policing
   D. Aggressive preventive patrol

4. In their work on personality and crime, Glueck and Glueck identified a number of personality traits that they believed characterized antisocial youth. Which of the following is NOT one of these?

   A. Narcissism
   B. Introversion
   C. Sadism
   D. Impulsiveness

5. Early problems with the first local police departments in the United States were most clearly due to

   A. lack of formal training
   B. unclear statutes concerning private property
   C. an abundance of non-police functions
   D. supervision by elected political officials

6. The earliest treatment programs used in United States prisons tended to be

   A. structured psychological treatments
   B. vocational
   C. educational
   D. informal counseling

7. Which of the following statements is in line with a criminal defendant's right to be free from *double jeopardy*?
   I. If a defendant is tried and convicted of murder in New York, he cannot be tried again for the same murder in New York.
   II. If a defendant is tried in federal court for a crime, he cannot be tried in state court for the same crime.
   III. If a single act violates the laws of two states, the offender may only be punished by one of the states.

   The CORRECT answer is:

   A. I only   B. II only   C. I, III   D. II, III

21

8. A state of normlessness in society, which may be caused by decreased homogeneity and which provides a setting conducive to crimes and other antisocial acts, is known as

   A. anomie   B. discord   C. inequity   D. ennui

9. Which of the following events would occur earliest in the cycle of *secondary deviance* as proposed by Edwin Lemert?

   A. Offense escalation
   B. Assumption of deviant identity
   C. Deviant self-labeling
   D. Legal reprisals

10. The first privately-run state prison in the United States was opened in Marion, Kentucky in

    A. 1941   B. 1968   C. 1975   D. 1986

11. A _____, granted by the president or state governor, is an exercise of the extraordinary power to change a criminal punishment to one less severe.

    A. commutation of sentence   B. reprieve
    C. pardon   D. set-aside judgment

12. Which of the following is a document filed in juvenile court alleging that a juvenile is a delinquent, a status offender, or a dependent, and asking that the juvenile be transferred to a criminal court for prosecution as an adult?

    A. Charge document   B. Petition
    C. Indictment   D. Disposition

13. Approximately what percentage of United States prison inmates have had a history of substance abuse?

    A. 20   B. 40   C. 60   D. 80

14. Which of the following are rulings made by the Supreme Court concerning a criminal defendant's right to a trial by a jury?
    I. When a 12-person jury is used, the Sixth Amendment does not require a unanimous verdict, except in first-degree murder cases.
    II. A 6-person jury will fulfill a defendant's right to trial by jury.
    III. In all capital cases, a 12-person jury must be used and the verdict must be unanimous.

    The CORRECT answer is:

    A. I *only*   B. III *only*   C. I, II   D. II, III

15. The branch of social science that uses the scientific method of the natural sciences, and which suggests that human behavior is a product of social, biological, psychological, or economic forces, is called

    A. animism   B. positivism
    C. syncretism   D. behaviorism

16. In prisons, the most traditional type of inmate treatment involves 16._____

    A. vocational rehabilitation
    B. educational programs
    C. private industry
    D. psychological counseling and therapy

17. Approximately what percentage of robberies in the United States are stranger-to- 17._____
    stranger crimes?

    A. 10   B. 30   C. 50   D. 75

18. Which of the following is NOT generally considered to be a weakness associated with 18._____
    United States juvenile courts today?

    A. A generalized lack of resources
    B. Problems created by the diversity of the courts' roles
    C. A reputation for dealing too harshly with young offenders
    D. The inferior position most juvenile courts hold in the court hierarchy

19. The process perspective of crime focuses on the _____ forces involved in influencing 19._____
    criminal behavior.

    A. situational   B. socialization
    C. economic/political   D. ecological

20. The right to _____ has undergone the most modification in the relatively recent proliferation 20._____
    of child-abuse cases in United States courts.

    A. be free from double jeopardy
    B. confront witnesses
    C. legal counsel
    D. a speedy and public trial

21. In general, the _____ is considered to be the core element of the American criminal justice 21._____
    system.

    A. criminal court   B. sheriff's department
    C. Supreme Court   D. corrections system

22. In recent years, _____ crimes have overtaken other forms of crime in terms of the number 22._____
    of court commitments in the United States.

    A. violent   B. public-order
    C. property   D. drug

23. A person in the United States who is convicted of a felony offense loses all civil rights. 23._____
    The term for this loss is

    A. attainder   B. divestiture
    C. disenfranchisement   D. rejoinder

24. The Safe Streets and Crime Control Act of _____ provided for the expenditure of federal 24._____
    funds for state and local crime control efforts.

    A. 1948   B. 1968   C. 1981   D. 1988

25. Which of the following was a United States penal reformer who introduced the idea of releasing prisoners once they had been reformed? 25._____

    A. August Vollmer
    B. Robert Peel
    C. Zebulon Brockway
    D. Walter Crofton

KEY (CORRECT ANSWERS)

1.	C	11.	A
2.	C	12.	B
3.	B	13.	D
4.	B	14.	C
5.	D	15.	B
6.	C	16.	D
7.	A	17.	D
8.	A	18.	C
9.	C	19.	B
10.	D	20.	B

21. A
22. D
23. A
24. B
25. C

EXAMINATION SECTION
TEST 1

DIRECTIONS: Each question or incomplete statement is followed by several suggested answers or completions. Select the one that BEST answers the question or completes the statement. *PRINT THE LETTER OF THE CORRECT ANSWER IN THE SPACE AT THE RIGHT.*

1. Most research that has been conducted on the issue of rehabilitating criminals in the United States has revealed that
    A. rehabilitation efforts are more likely to work if an offender receives individual attention from the system
    B. in general, rehabilitation efforts have no appreciable effect on recidivism
    C. rehabilitation through the medical model has proven to be slightly more effective than vocational or educational programs
    D. offenders who go through some type of rehabilitation program are not nearly as likely to recidivate as offenders who are merely incarcerated

2. Unlawfully obtaining, or attempting to obtain the property of another by the threat of eventual injury or harm to that person, the person's property, or another person is an offense classified officially as
    A. extortion
    B. aggravated assault
    C. terrorism
    D. blackmail

3. The current explanation for female crime in the United States focuses on
    A. the *chivalry hypothesis* of hidden female crime
    B. the social role of women in society
    C. the *masculinity hypothesis* of females who commit crime
    D. economic status

4. Which of the following crimes generally has no statute of limitations?
    A. Robbery
    B. Murder
    C. Rape
    D. Embezzlement

5. In general, proponents of the due process model of criminal justice tend to be
    A. representatives of the business lobby
    B. members of the legal profession who see themselves as protectors of civil rights
    C. members of the legal profession who vigorously prosecute criminal offenses
    D. victims of violent crime

6. Which of the following principles is NOT included in a nonintervention justice philosophy?
    A. Decarceration
    B. Rehabilitation
    C. Diversion
    D. Decriminalization

7. Which of the following views of crime asserts that offenses can be expected if there is a suitable target that is not protected by capable guardians? The
    A. rational choice view
    B. medical model
    C. developmental view
    D. routine activities view

8. The charge of second-degree murder requires the actor to have

   A. premeditation
   B. dissent
   C. deliberation
   D. malice aforethought

9. In the United States correctional system, probationary sentences are granted by each of the following EXCEPT _____ courts.

   A. state superior
   B. state district
   C. municipal
   D. federal district

10. Each of the following factors has been shown to have a direct correlation to the incidence of spouse abuse EXCEPT

    A. education level
    B. the presence of alcohol
    C. military service
    D. economic stress

11. Which of the following occurs at the latest stage in the criminal justice process?

    A. Bail considered
    B. Arraignment
    C. Plea negotiations
    D. Custody

12. Some critics of the American criminal justice system argue that it is a political entity that operates subjectively, with some cases receiving the full attention of the law, while others are settled with a minimum of due process. This idea is known as the _____ model of justice.

    A. caste
    B. wedding cake
    C. medical
    D. Marxist

13. Which of the following is characteristic of a *watchman* style of policing?

    A. Formal authority both within the department and between officers and the public
    B. An emphasis on community relations
    C. Low turnover
    D. Relatively infrequent arrests

14. Which of the following is/are considered to be serious limitations or drawbacks associated with the use of self-report studies for measuring crime?
    I. Their accuracy in determining the behavior of chronic offenders
    II. Their accuracy in determining the behavior of persistent drug abusers
    III. Their validity and reliability in measuring youth crimes

    The CORRECT answer is:

    A. I only
    B. II only
    C. I, II
    D. II, III

15. Each of the following is considered a factor that would render a punishment of a criminal *cruel and unusual* and therefore unconstitutional EXCEPT

    A. it shocks the general conscience and is fundamentally unfair
    B. the punishment degrades the dignity of human beings
    C. it involves physical discomfort or mental uncertainty
    D. it is more severe than the offense for which it has been given

16. Which of the following is NOT typically a responsibility assigned to a correctional officer? 16.____

    A. Protecting inmates from other inmates
    B. Preventing escapes
    C. Making sure inmates are adequately fed
    D. Controlling inmate movement within the institution

17. In a typical state judicial system, the highest court with general jurisdiction may be called by any of the names below EXCEPT 17.____

    A. superior court
    B. court of common pleas
    C. intermediate appellate court
    D. circuit court

18. What is the term for a written order issued by a judicial officer that requires a person accused of a criminal offense to appear in a designated court at a specified time to answer the charges? 18.____

    A. Indictment   B. Summons
    C. Injunction   D. Subpoena

19. The _____ theory of crime states that material goals pervade all aspects of American life, and therefore crime rates are high in American culture. 19.____

    A. institutional anomie   B. focal concern
    C. behavioral   D. relative deprivation

20. The logical argument behind the concept of _____ is that as long as criminals are in prison, they cannot be on the streets committing crimes. 20.____

    A. conditional release   B. incapacitation
    C. restitution   D. deterrence

21. What is the term for the legal principle by which the decision or holding in an earlier case becomes the standard by which subsequent similar cases are judged? 21.____

    A. Presentment   B. Caveat emptor
    C. Summation   D. Stare decisis

22. As an alternative to bail in some courts, a criminal defendant is released with no immediate requirement of payment. However, if the defendant fails to appear, he or she is liable for the full amount.
    This system is known as 22.____

    A. deposit bail   B. surety bail
    C. unsecured bail   D. conditional release

23. A common pathway to crime begins at an early age with stubborn behavior and defiance of parents. These behaviors lead to defiance and disobedience, and then to authority avoidances such as truancy or running away.
    This is known as the _____ pathway. 23.____

    A. classical   B. overt
    C. covert   D. authority conflict

24. According to most research, the rearrest rate for prison inmates who are paroled in the United States is about _____ percent.

    A. 30   B. 45   C. 60   D. 90

25. The exclusionary rule in criminal justice proceedings is based upon the rights granted in the _____ Amendment to the Constitution.

    A. First   B. Second   C. Fourth   D. Fifth

KEY (CORRECT ANSWERS)

1.	B	11.	C
2.	A	12.	B
3.	D	13.	D
4.	B	14.	C
5.	B	15.	C
6.	B	16.	C
7.	D	17.	C
8.	D	18.	B
9.	C	19.	A
10.	A	20.	B

21. D
22. C
23. D
24. C
25. C

TEST 2

DIRECTIONS: Each question or incomplete statement is followed by several suggested answers or completions. Select the one that BEST answers the question or completes the statement. *PRINT THE LETTER OF THE CORRECT ANSWER IN THE SPACE AT THE RIGHT.*

1. The recidivism rate of probationers in the United States is _____ than the recidivism rate of prison inmates.

    A. much higher
    B. somewhat higher
    C. somewhat lower
    D. much lower

2. To prove that a murder has taken place, most state jurisdictions require prosecutors to prove that the accused

    A. was provoked into a crime of passion
    B. intentionally and with malice desired the death of the victim
    C. understood at the time of the murder that killing was wrong
    D. was of sound mind when the crime occurred

3. What is the term for the process in which a potential jury panel is questioned by the prosecution and defense to select jurors who are unbiased and objective?

    A. Nolle prosequi
    B. Voir dire
    C. Venire
    D. Peremptory challenge

4. Approximately how many law enforcement agencies are administered by the United States government?

    A. 6   B. 18   C. 35   D. 50

5. The idea that criminal acts are related to a person's exposure to an excess amount of antisocial attitudes and values is known as the principle of

    A. differential association
    B. interactionism
    C. deinstitutionalization
    D. degenerate anomalies

6. Which of the following would NOT typically be classified as a status offense?

    A. Shoplifting
    B. Curfew violation
    C. Possession of alcohol
    D. Truancy

7. In which of the following court cases was it ruled that the death penalty may be applied when aggravating circumstances exist in a murder case, such as murder for profit?

    A. Powell v. Alabama (1932)
    B. Benton v. Maryland (1969)
    C. Gregg v. Georgia (1981)
    D. Rhodes v. Chapman (1981)

8. Which of the following was a utilitarian philosopher whose works helped spawn the classical theory of criminal behavior?

    A. Karl Marx
    B. Cesare Beccaria
    C. Emile Durkheim
    D. Enrico Ferri

9. State sentencing codes usually include various factors that can legitimately influence the length of prison sentences. Which of the following is NOT one of these factors?

   A. The offender's prior criminal record
   B. Whether the offender used weapons
   C. Whether the crime was committed for money
   D. The offender's economic status

10. Research on the prison culture in today's correctional institutions has revealed each of the following EXCEPT

    A. newer inmates tend to be younger than before and disdainful of older inmates
    B. white inmates are much more cohesively organized than black or Latin inmates
    C. more inmates than ever are assigned to protective custody
    D. those who adapt best to the prison culture are the least likely to reform on the outside

11. In the crime of larceny, a victim willingly gives up temporary possession of property, but retains legal ownership. This is known as

    A. constructive intent
    B. custodial convenience
    C. noncoercive larceny
    D. constructive possession

12. In most local police departments, the majority of officers are assigned to

    A. identifying public-order crimes
    B. traffic control
    C. patrol work
    D. investigations

13. Which of the following offers the best example to a *good faith exception* to the exclusionary rule?

    A. The police use of overflights to spy on marijuana growers without the use of a warrant
    B. The unauthorized taping, by a civilian, of a telephone conversation involving a second party who is unaware that the conversation is being recorded
    C. The coercion of a confession from a violent killer who is a flight risk
    D. A stop-and-frisk of persons outside a building that is known to house a drug operation, without the use of a warrant

14. People who favor the death penalty in America, and yet criticize its failure to act as a real deterrent, usually focus their criticism on the _____ of the punishment.

    A. severity
    B. certainty
    C. privacy
    D. swiftness

15. A criminal court whose trial jurisdiction includes no felonies, and which may or may not hear appeals, is known as a court of _____ jurisdiction.

    A. limited   B. appellate   C. criminal   D. general

16. Which of the following statements about local police investigations is true? 16._____
    A. Suspects are usually identified before a detective is assigned to a case.
    B. The majority of solved cases involved the gathering of data and evidence by detectives away from the crime scene.
    C. Detectives spend an average of 2-5 days on each case.
    D. A mastery of investigative techniques is usually the most significant element involved in solving crimes.

17. The primary goal of intensive probation supervision as a means of correction is 17._____
    A. reintegration   B. punishment
    C. diversion   D. control

18. What is the term for a government agency or subunit that receives and screens juvenile referrals from police, or from other agencies or persons? 18._____
    A. Booking room   B. Intake unit
    C. Disposition unit   D. Diagnosis center

19. Which of the following types of treatment, administered to prison inmates, uses tokens to reward conformity and develop positive behavior traits? 19._____
    A. Reality therapy   B. Behavior therapy
    C. Transactional analysis D. Social therapy

20. Forcible rape is coerced 20._____
    I.   sexual intercourse induced by the threat of social, economic, or vocational harm
    II. participation of a male in intercourse or other sexual activity by a female
    III. sexual intercourse induced by the threat of physical harm
    IV. participation in oral sex
    The CORRECT answer is:
    A. I only   B. I, II, III   C. III only   D. III, IV

21. Within the criminal justice system, the _____ typically represent the first step in deterring crime. 21._____
    A. police   B. prosecution
    C. communities   D. correctional officers

22. Which of the following individuals has been credited with pioneering the concept of probation? 22._____
    A. August Vollmer   B. Cesare Beccaria
    C. Karl Marx   D. John Augustus

23. In the majority of states, state court judges are selected 23._____
    A. by an executive council elected by the state assembly
    B. through popular election
    C. by the state senate
    D. by means of gubernatorial appointment

24. Which of the following factors is LEAST likely to be correlated with the crime of child abuse?

    A. Family isolation
    B. Parents with little or no secondary or higher-level education
    C. Familial stress
    D. Parents who have suffered abuse

25. The criticism currently leveled against the practice of parole in the United States includes each of the following arguments EXCEPT

    A. the process has the unintended effect of granting an inmate too much power and control over the path his or her future may take
    B. it is beyond the capacity of parole authorities to predict who will make a successful judgment on parole, or to accurately monitor their behavior in the community
    C. the procedures that control the decision to grant parole are vague and have not been controlled by due process considerations
    D. it is unjust to decide whether to release an individual from prison based on what we expect that person to do in the future

KEY (CORRECT ANSWERS)

1.	C	11.	D
2.	B	12.	C
3.	B	13.	A
4.	D	14.	B
5.	A	15.	A
6.	A	16.	A
7.	C	17.	C
8.	B	18.	B
9.	D	19.	B
10.	B	20.	C

21.	A
22.	D
23.	B
24.	B
25.	A

EXAMINATION SECTION
TEST 1

DIRECTIONS: Each question or incomplete statement is followed by several suggested answers or completions. Select the one that BEST answers the question or completes the statement. *PRINT THE LETTER OF THE CORRECT ANSWER IN THE SPACE AT THE RIGHT.*

1. In BLACK'S LAW DICTIONARY, the following definition appears: ..."*such an exercise of the powers of government as the settled maxims of the law permit and sanction, and under such safeguards for the protection of individual rights as those maxims prescribe for the class of cases to which the one in question belongs.*"
What is defined above?

   A. Judicial restraint
   B. The exclusionary rule
   C. Due process
   D. Good faith

2. The _____ theory of the nature of crime combines elements of sociological and psychological theories.

   A. interactional
   B. cognitive
   C. human nature
   D. social development

3. During the nineteenth century, the state of New York developed a prison system that stressed congregate working conditions. The name for this system was

   A. curtilage
   B. the Auburn system
   C. the Peel system
   D. chancery

4. In most adult courts, the plea bargaining process occurs between

   A. setting bail and releasing or detaining the accused
   B. reading the charge and setting bail
   C. arrest and arraignment
   D. arraignment and the onset of trial

5. In the United States, criminal justice agencies have existed for about _____ years.

   A. 250   B. 200   C. 150   D. 100

6. Through the process of _____, a judicial officer orders that an adjudicated and sentenced adult be admitted into a correctional facility.

   A. adjudication
   B. sentencing
   C. arraignment
   D. commitment

7. The onset of professionalism in American police work can most clearly be traced to the influence of

   A. Cesare Beccaria
   B. August Vollmer
   C. Robert Peel
   D. J. Edgar Hoover

8. The _____ model is a view of corrections that holds that convicted offenders are victims of their environment who need care and treatment to be transformed into valuable members of society.

   A. developmental
   B. medical
   C. principle of impulsivity
   D. interactional

9. According to the Bureau of Justice Statistics, White offenders in the United States are more likely than Black offenders to be incarcerated for crimes involving

    A. drugs   B. weapons   C. property   D. violence

10. Which of the following is a provision of the Crime Control Act of 1990?

    A. Expanded criminal asset forfeiture laws
    B. Increased federal criminal penalties for drug offenses
    C. Added designer drugs to the drug schedule
    D. Sanctioned anabolic steroids

11. Which of the following is a fact that jeopardizes the validity of the entire concept of deterrence?

    A. Police crackdowns have proven ineffective at quelling large-scale operations such as fences.
    B. The death penalty has not been shown to deter violent crime.
    C. The effect of arrest as a deterrent is usually race-specific.
    D. The impact of deterrent measures on alcohol-impaired driving is negligible over the long term.

12. Currently, female inmates make up about _____ percent of the United States prison population.

    A. 5   B. 15   C. 25   D. 40

13. Each of the following is a significant difference between today's juvenile and adult court systems EXCEPT

    A. juvenile hearings are more informal
    B. juvenile hearings rely more on anecdotal, rather than clinical or social evidence
    C. rules of evidence are more strictly adhered to in adult courts
    D. the standard of proof – guilty beyond a reasonable doubt – is not always adhered to in juvenile court

14. The _____ perspective on the study of crime focuses on the economic and political forces involved in criminal behavior.

    A. integrated   B. conflict
    C. classical   D. biological/psychological

15. For criminals, the most important factors that deter criminal behavior are those that

    A. are most severe in their sanction
    B. are in the visible present
    C. cause the greatest amount of physical pain
    D. are most widely publicized

16. Due process rights include each of the following EXCEPT the right to

    A. have favorable witnesses appear   B. be present at trial
    C. free speech   D. confront hostile witnesses

17. In what region of the United States are most executions carried out?   17._____

    A. West   B. Midwest   C. South   D. Northeast

18. A sentencing structure that provides the time an average sentence should be served,   18._____
    along with the option of extending or decreasing the punishment because of aggravating
    or mitigating circumstances, is described as

    A. presumptive   B. indeterminate
    C. mandatory   D. peremptory

19. The function of a(n) _____ is to match individualized, rehabilitative diagnosis of a juve-   19._____
    nile offender with effective community supervision.

    A. juvenile defender   B. juvenile probation officer
    C. intake officer   D. juvenile court judge

20. The Differential _____ theory explains criminal behavior by using the perspectives of   20._____
    others in determining one's own choices of behavior.

    A. Identification   B. Association Reinforcement
    C. Anticipation   D. Association

21. In a typical juvenile justice process, the adjudication hearing takes place between the   21._____

    A. intake prescreening and detention hearing
    B. detention hearing and intake
    C. intake and arraignment hearing
    D. arraignment hearing and disposition hearing

22. Most probation agencies in the United States are _____ level agencies.   22._____

    A. municipal   B. county   C. state   D. federal

23. A general term for an order of a superior court commanding that a lower court, adminis-   23._____
    trative body, or executive body perform a specific function is called a writ of

    A. execution   B. habeas corpus
    C. certiorari   D. mandamus

24. Which of the following social process theories of crime attempts to explain why so many   24._____
    juvenile delinquents do not become adult criminals?
    _____ theory.

    A. Differential Association   B. Neutralization
    C. Differential Reinforcement   D. Containment

25. Each of the following variables is considered to be basic to the study of the deterrence of   25._____
    criminal behavior EXCEPT

    A. rehabilitation   B. severity of punishment
    C. certainty of punishment   D. swiftness of punishment

KEY (CORRECT ANSWERS)

1. C
2. A
3. B
4. D
5. C

6. D
7. B
8. B
9. B
10. D

11. B
12. A
13. B
14. B
15. B

16. C
17. C
18. A
19. B
20. A

21. D
22. C
23. D
24. B
25. A

TEST 2

DIRECTIONS: Each question or incomplete statement is followed by several suggested answers or completions. Select the one that BEST answers the question or completes the statement. *PRINT THE LETTER OF THE CORRECT ANSWER IN THE SPACE AT THE RIGHT.*

1. Which Amendment to the Constitution states that a person has the right to be represented by legal counsel at a criminal trial?   1._____

   A. Third   B. Fifth   C. Sixth   D. Eighth

2. Which of the following statements about the role of local police in deterring crime is generally FALSE?   2._____

   A. Police have proven effective at deterring crime by patroling enclosed environments such as subway cars or stations.
   B. Ordinary police car patrol deters very little if any crime.
   C. An officer on foot patrol has not proven to deter more crime than no patrol at all.
   D. The cost of police relative to the financial costs of the crimes they deter is very high.

3. Which of the following demographic correlates of crime is most generally universal; i.e., its effects on crime are independent of other demographics, and its effect on crime is consistently correlated?   3._____

   A. Gender   B. Education
   C. Economic status   D. Age

4. Since 1980, the prison population in the United States has increased by approximately _____ percent.   4._____

   A. 30   B. 90   C. 120   D. 170

5. If true, the theory that state executions of killers may actually increase the likelihood of murder is an illustration of the   5._____

   A. Hawthorne effect   B. wergild
   C. brutalization effect   D. conflict perspective

6. The due process movement in American criminal justice reached its peak during the era in which the Supreme Court was led by Chief Justice   6._____

   A. Frederick Vinson   B. Earl Warren
   C. Warren Burger   D. William Rehnquist

7. In the history of corrections, the philosophy of the _____ was crime prevention through fear of punishment and silent confinement.   7._____

   A. Auburn System   B. Newgate Prison
   C. Contract System   D. Western Penitentiary

8. In some states, probate court, a special court that handles wills, administration of estates, and guardianship of minors and incompetents, is known as _____ court.   8._____

   A. surrogate   B. common pleas
   C. domestic relations D. circuit

37

9. A prosecutor's formal written accusation that a specified person has committed a specified offense, laid before a grand jury to be found true and filed in a court, is known as a(n)

   A. indictment
   B. charge document
   C. complaint
   D. arraignment

10. The _____ model of criminal justice in the United States holds that the practice of parole is ineffective and should be abolished.

    A. radical
    B. non-intervention
    C. justice
    D. crime control

11. The major premise of the left realism theory of crime is that

    A. crime is a function of relative deprivation, and criminals tend to prey on the poor
    B. criminals are revolutionaries
    C. peace and humanism can reduce crime
    D. the capital system creates a patriarchy which oppresses women

12. Approximately what percentage of United States prison inmates have been incarcerated prior to their current term?

    A. 20
    B. 40
    C. 60
    D. 90

13. The area of law referring to civil wrongs is known as _____ law.

    A. tort
    B. case
    C. fiduciary
    D. public

14. Which of the following theories of crime attempts to explain irrational violence?

    A. General theory of deviance
    B. Biochemical
    C. Neutralization theory
    D. Evolutionary

15. Which of the following explains criminal behavior based on the idea that social isolation reduces an individual's perception of available behavior alternatives so that criminal activity is then seen as a way to reduce the tensions of isolation?

    A. Anomie
    B. Closure theory
    C. Differential Association theory
    D. Determinism

16. Many people reject goals and standards that seem impossible to achieve, such as going to college. This is known as

    A. mental set
    B. reaction formation
    C. antisocial passivity
    D. cognitive dissonance

17. The concept of substantive due process may be invoked in the criminal justice system today to rule that

    A. a defendant has a right to legal counsel
    B. criminal statutes may be unconstitutional because they are vague or arbitrary
    C. a person is protected from unreasonable search and seizure
    D. a defendant has a right to an appellate review procedure

18. In the United States criminal justice system, approximately what percentage of criminal 18.____
    defendants are released on bail?

    A. 10 B. 40 C. 65 D. 80

19. When a criminal or juvenile justice agency signifies that a portion of the justice process is 19.____
    complete and that jurisdiction has been relinquished or transferred to another agency,
    _____ has occurred.

    A. disposition B. adjudication
    C. diversion D. dismissal

20. Which of the following motivations for punishing criminal behavior is NOT based on prac- 20.____
    tical concerns?

    A. Deterrence B. Retribution
    C. Incapacitation D. Rehabilitation

21. Which of the following United States geographical regions reports the highest incidence 21.____
    of rape?

    A. South B. West C. Midwest D. Northeast

22. Most jurisdictions in the United States have a standard set of rules governing the terms 22.____
    of probation. Which of the following is LEAST likely to be one of these rules?

    A. Maintaining steady employment
    B. Submitting to electronic monitoring
    C. Meeting family responsibilities
    D. Making restitution for loss or damage

23. The major premise of Sellin's culture conflict theory of crime is that 23.____

    A. obedience to the norms of the lower class culture puts people into conflict with the
       norms of the dominant culture
    B. status frustration of lower class boys causes them to join gangs
    C. crime occurs when the wealthy and the poor live in close proximity to each other
    D. blockage of conventional opportunities causes lower class youths to join criminal,
       conflict, or retreatist gangs

24. Each of the following is a trend associated with the modern era of corrections EXCEPT 24.____

    A. increasing violence within the system
    B. it has become more common to view the correctional system as a device for reha-
       bilitation and reform
    C. the retrenchment of *the prisoner's rights* movement
    D. the alleged failure of correctional rehabilitation has led many to reconsider the pur-
       pose of incapacitation

25. Recidivism is the term for the 25.____

    A. recycling of a person back into the criminal justice system
    B. mental regression of an offender into a childlike state
    C. repetition of criminal behavior
    D. failure to meet the conditions of a probation or parole

KEY (CORRECT ANSWERS)

1.	C		11.	A
2.	C		12.	C
3.	D		13.	A
4.	D		14.	B
5.	C		15.	B
6.	B		16.	B
7.	A		17.	B
8.	A		18.	C
9.	A		19.	A
10.	C		20.	B

21. B
22. B
23. A
24. B
25. C

EXAMINATION SECTION
TEST 1

DIRECTIONS: Each question or incomplete statement is followed by several suggested answers or completions. Select the one that BEST answers the question or completes the statement. *PRINT THE LETTER OF THE CORRECT ANSWER IN THE SPACE AT THE RIGHT.*

1. The conditions under which the law, following the M'Naghten case, considers an individual insane include a person who
    I. does not know his own name
    II. is suffering from autism
    III. is extremely anti-social
    IV. doesn't know the nature and quality of the act he/she does
    V. doesn't know that the act was wrong
   The CORRECT answer is:

   A. I only   B. I, II, IV   C. IV only   D. IV, V   E. I, IV, V

2. The purpose of the insanity defense is to
    I. allow insane people to commit crimes
    II. provide defense attorneys with a last resort
    III. render some individuals not legally responsible
    IV. protect society against insane people
    V. mitigate blame
   The CORRECT answer is:

   A. IV only   B. I, II, V   C. III, V   D. IV, V
   E. None of the above

3. People who commit a crime while suffering a delusion are
    I. legally insane
    II. able to offer an insanity defense
    III. medically insane
    IV. to be treated as normal
    V. treated exactly like other criminals
   The CORRECT answer is:

   A. I, II, V   B. III only   C. II only   D. V only   E. III, V

4. To judge whether a delusory defendant is to be excused or not, we must
    I. understand what his delusion was at the time of the crime
    II. make sure he is coherent during his trial
    III. decide whether his act would have been justified if his delusion were real
    IV. decide whether a reasonable person would suffer from a similar delusion
    V. judge his act within the context of the delusion
   The CORRECT answer is:

   A. I, II, III   B. IV only   C. II, IV   D. I, III, V
   E. All of the above

5. Under the law, a defendant whose act was committed under an "uncontrollable impulse of the mind" can
    I. *claim* the insanity defense in general
    II. *claim* mitigatory circumstances
    III. *claim* a partial insanity defense
    IV. *always claim* temporary insanity even if he knew what he was doing
    V. *not claim* a legal defense on insanity grounds
   The CORRECT answer is:

   A. I, II   B. V *only*   C. III *only*   D. IV *only*   E. I, II, III, IV

6. According to legal standards, "moral insanity" refers to that condition in which a
    I. person's intellectual and moral faculties are sound but are ignored due to anger or passion
    II. person's moral faculties are sound but his intellectual faculties are impaired
    III. person's intellectual faculties are sound but his moral faculties are impaired
    IV. person's moral and intellectual faculties are unsound
    V. person displays psychotic tendencies
   The CORRECT answer is:

   A. I *only*   B. II *only*   C. III *only*   D. IV *only*   E. V *only*

7. The concept of punishment is
    I. morally neutral
    II. capable of scientific scrutiny
    III. legally definable
    IV. one that exists in a complex institutional structure
    V. incompletely accepted by criminologists
   The CORRECT answer is:

   A. I, II   B. III, IV   C. III *only*   D. I, II, III
   E. All of the above

8. A(The) concept(s) shared by law and morality is(are):
    I. Fairness
    II. Justification
    III. Culpability
    IV. prosecution
    V. Indictment
   The CORRECT answer is:

   A. I, II   B. III, IV   C. I, III, V   D. II *only*
   E. All of the above

9. The criminological field of the "disposition of offenders" covers
    I. indicted felons only
    II. all who are arrested
    III. those brought to trial and acquitted
    IV. those brought to trial and convicted
    V. all those who are indicted
   The CORRECT answer is:

   A. I *only*   B. II, III   C. II, IV   D. IV *only*
   E. All of the above

10. Different schools of thought in the field of punishment theory include:
    I. Legal positivism
    II. Retributivism
    III. Rehabilitationism
    IV. Natural law theory
    V. Behaviorism
    The CORRECT answer is:

    A. I, IV, V   B. I, II, IV   C. II, III   D. I, II, III, V
    E. All of the above

11. In criminology, the concept of "recidivism" refers to
    I. processing the criminally insane
    II. using statistics to measure crime
    III. rates of re-conviction
    IV. police abuse of records and data
    V. the modus operandi
    The CORRECT answer is:

    A. I only   B. II, IV, V   C. III only   D. II, III, IV   E. III, V

12. One(The) problem(s) seriously affecting the study of criminology is(are) that
    I. it seriously overlaps with sociology and law
    II. it has a relatively short history
    III. so few comprehensive texts exist
    IV. most people don't know what it is
    V. its subject matter is complex
    The CORRECT answer is:

    A. I only   B. II, III, V   C. I, IV, V   D. I, III, IV, V
    E. All of the above

13. For students of criminology, problems are created by the
    I. relative complexity of the criminal justice system
    II. relative independence of various parts of the criminal justice system
    III. lack of coordination among the various sub-systems in the criminal justice system
    IV. faculty members who have sociology degrees
    V. popular misconceptions about crime
    The CORRECT answer is:

    A. I, II   B. I, II, III, V   C. III, IV, V   D. III, IV
    E. All of the above

14. The rehabilitative approach to punishment, as opposed to the retributive, emphasizes
    I. crimes rather than criminals
    II. criminals rather than crimes
    III. offenders rather than offenses
    IV. the future rather than the past
    V. the past rather than the future
    The CORRECT answer is:

    A. I, IV, V   B. II, III, IV   C. I only   D. I, II   E. I, II, V

15. A(The) generally objective charge(s) frequently made *against* punishment is(are) that
    I. it should be left to God alone
    II. laws are too vague
    III. it is really camouflaged revenge
    IV. it is too slow
    V. it is too lenient
    The CORRECT answer is:

    A. I, II   B. IV *only*   C. II, IV   D. III *only*   E. I, II, II

16. Criminological theories, like other scientific theories, must meet certain criteria, such as:
    I. Objectivity
    II. Verifiability
    III. Falsifiability
    IV. Publicity
    V. Coherence
    The CORRECT answer is:

    A. I, II, III   B. I, II, III, V   C. III, IV, V   D. I *only*
    E. All of the above

17. Together with other social sciences, the study of criminology differs from that of the natural sciences in that
    I. what it studies is very vague
    II. its subject is human beings
    III. the objects of its research are subjects
    IV. the researchers doing it form part of its subject matter
    V. consensus is easily achieved
    The CORRECT answer is:

    A. I, II, V   B. I, III, V   C. I, II, III   D. II, III, IV
    E. None of the above

18. The fields of intellectual endeavor that are irrelevant to criminology are:
    I. Law
    II. Sociology
    III. Psychology
    IV. Philosophy
    V. Jurisprudence
    The CORRECT answer is:

    A. II, IV, V   B. I, II, V   C. I, II, III, V   D. I, II, III, IV
    E. I, III, IV

19. A (The) *major* critic(s) of rehabilitative theory is(are):
    I. Dr. Karl Menninger
    II. Eric Fromm
    III. Dr. Thomas Szasz
    IV. Justice Burger
    V. C. Wright Mills
    The CORRECT answer is:

    A. II, IV   B. I, II   C. III *only*   D. IV, V   E. I, V

5 (#1)

20. The MAIN claim(s) of the rehabilitative approach to punishment is(are) that it is :
    I. less expensive
    II. more humane
    III. more rational
    IV. fairer
    V. more effective
    The CORRECT answer is:

    A. I, III, V   B. II only   C. II, IV, V   D. III only
    E. All of the above

21. The *majority* of criminals are actually
    I. misguided
    II. misled
    III. unfortunate
    IV. poor
    V. unintelligent
    The CORRECT answer is:

    A. I, II, V   B. III only   C. IV only   D. II, III   E. IV, V

22. The *earliest* forms of prisons were designed to
    I. protect others from the inmates
    II. cure the inmates
    III. reform the inmates
    IV. quarantine the insane
    V. house the homeless
    The CORRECT answer is:

    A. I, II, V   B. I, III, V   C. I, IV   D. III only   E. IV only

23. A relatively recently proposed reform of concern to criminologists
    I. would abolish judges
    II. advocates plea bargaining
    III. attempts to avoid plea bargaining
    IV. compensates victims
    V. re-institutes the death penalty
    The CORRECT answer is:

    A. I, II, V   B. I, III, V   C. I, IV   D. IV only
    E. None of the above

24. A (The) *major* difference (s) between rehabilitative and retributionist judges is(are):
    I. The former give determinate sentences
    II. The latter give determinate sentences
    III. The former consider the future more than the past
    IV. The latter consider the future more than the past
    V. Only one prefers indeterminate sentences
    The CORRECT answer is:

    A. I, II, V   B. II, IV   C. I only   D. II, V   E. II, III, V

25. Old laws which have not yet been taken off the books are *popularly* called:
    I. stupid
    II. illegal
    III. supererogatory
    IV. blue
    V. white
    The CORRECT answer is:

    A. I, III   B. II, V   C. IV *only*   D. I, III, IV   E. V *only*

26. To the rehabilitationist, the criminal is *probably*
    I. in need of medical services
    II. sick
    III. bad
    IV. in need of financial help
    V. sadistic
    The CORRECT answer is:

    A. I, II   B. II, III   C. I, IV, V   D. II, IV, V   E. I, III

27. To the retributionist, the criminal is *probably*
    I. in need of medical services
    II. sick
    III. bad
    IV. in need of financial help
    V. sadistic
    The CORRECT answer is:

    A. I, II   B. II, III   C. I, IV   D. II, IV, V   E. III, IV

28. A *necessary* condition for punishment is:
    I. Actus reus
    II. Mens rea
    III. Committing a crime
    IV. Contemplating a crime
    V. A witness
    The CORRECT answer is:

    A. I, II, V   B. II, IV   C. I, III   D. I *only*   E. I, II, III, IV

29. One (The) problem(s) caused by the complexity of the criminal justice system in American criminal procedure is(are):
    I. The constitution guarantees a speedy trial
    II. Cases get lost in red tape
    III. Courts are overloaded with cases
    IV. Everyone is guaranteed a lawyer
    V. Courts appoint attorneys
    The CORRECT answer is:

    A. I, II   B. II, III   C. I *only*   D. IV *only*   E. I, V

30. A (The) characteristic(s) of the "anomie" theory of criminology is(are) that, according to this theory criminals are
    I. those who cause problems for others
    II. social deviants
    III. those who disobey the law
    IV. whoever the police say they are
    V. rational
    The CORRECT answer is:

    A. I, II, V   B. II, III, V   C. I, III   D. I only   E. II only

31. One (The) disadvantage(s) of the "anomie" theory of criminology is(are) that it ignores
    I. white collar criminals
    II. blue collar criminals
    III. law-abiding eccentrics
    IV. women
    V. socialization
    The CORRECT answer is:

    A. I, II   B. I, III   C. IV only   D. III only   E. III, V

32. A *primary* feature of criminal punishment is that
    I. it provides a form of social control
    II. it cannot be morally justified
    III. no one knows whether he/she will be involved in it
    IV. it is institutionalized
    V. it is inconsistently enforced
    The CORRECT answer is:

    A. I only   B. II only   C. I, IV   D. IV, V   E. I, II, III

33. The concept of "equality" before the law means:
    I. Criminals are equally innocent
    II. Criminals are equally guilty
    III. People very unequal from others are exceptions
    IV. Some people are more equal than others
    V. Talents are equally distributed through society
    The CORRECT answer is:

    A. I only   B. II only   C. I, III   D. IV only   E. I, II, V

34. One (The) meaning(s) NOT intended by the concept of legal equality is(are) that most people
    I. are intellectually equal
    II. are physically equal
    III. have a roughly equal education
    IV. have equal opportunities
    V. have talents that are equally distributed through society
    The CORRECT answer is:

    A. I only   B. II only   C. I, II, V   D. I, II, III, IV
    E. All of the above

35. A(The) term(s) rarely, if ever, found in a rehabilitationist's vocabulary is(are):
    I. deserve
    II. merit
    III. justice
    IV. humane
    V. vindication
    The CORRECT answer is:

    A. I, IV   B. I, II   C. I, II, III   D. IV only   E. I, II, V

36. Both G.H.Mead and Emile Durkheim agree that, with respect to punishment theory,
    I. not all deviant acts are criminal acts
    II. not all criminal acts are harmful to the community
    III. all deviant acts are criminal acts
    IV. all criminal acts are harmful, in some way, to the community
    V. society is responsible for discontented citizens
    The CORRECT answer is:

    A. I, II, V   B. I, III   C. I, IV   D. I only   E. II only

37. The *major* problem(s) with equating criminal behavior with social deviance is(are) that
    I. social deviance is fun
    II. social deviance can create social stability
    III. social deviance creates social instability
    IV. criminals may be conformists
    V. crime sometimes pays
    The CORRECT answer is:

    A. I, II, V   B. II, III   C. I, IV   D. II, IV   E. II, IV, V

38. Non-violent crimes against the person include:
    I. Robbery
    II. Rape
    III. Burglary
    IV. Theft
    V. Libel
    The CORRECT answer is:

    A. I, II   B. I only   C. III, IV, V   D. III only   E. II, III, IV, V

39. Violent crimes against the person include:
    I. Robbery
    II. Rape
    III. Burglary
    IV. Theft
    V. Libel
    The CORRECT answer is:

    A. I, II   B. I only   C. III, IV, V   D. III only   E. II, III, IV, V

40. The *vast* majority of criminals serving time in America are
    I. innocent
    II. guilty
    III. men
    IV. women
    V. addicts
    The CORRECT answer is:

    A. I only   B. II only   C. II, IV, V   D. I, III, V   E. II, III

41. Most convicted offenders have the following characteristics:
    They
    I. come from rural areas
    II. come from urban areas
    III. are over 25
    IV. are under 25
    V. are mentally disturbed
    The CORRECT answer is:

    A. I, IV, V   B. II, IV   C. III only   D. I, II, III
    E. All of the above

42. Most persons convicted of crimes are those who
    I. acted rashly
    II. acted premeditatedly
    III. are employed
    IV. are unemployed
    V. acted unpremeditatedly
    The CORRECT answer is:

    A. I, IV   B. I, III   C. II, IV, V   D. IV only   E. II, IV

43. Most criminals are lacking in
    I. education
    II. ability
    III. fathers who live at home
    IV. nutrition
    V. common sense
    The CORRECT answer is:

    A. I only   B. I, II   C. II, III   D. I, IV   E. I, IV, V

44. Crimes frequently considered to be "victimless," include:
    I. Prostitution
    II. Gambling
    III. Auto theft
    IV. Shoplifting
    V. Embezzlement
    The CORRECT answer is:

    A. I only   B. I, II   C. I, IV   D. I, IV, V   E. I, II, V

45. One (The) problem(s) frequently cited concerning sentencing is that sentences
    I. differ for similar crimes
    II. differ for all crimes
    III. are uniform for various crimes
    IV. are avoided by plea bargaining
    V. are specified precisely by legislation
    The CORRECT answer is:

    A. I, IV, V   B. I, II, V   C. I, II, III   D. III only   E. I only

46. The problem(s) with the WARDEN'S SURVEY RESEARCH METHOD, i.e., the method in which the criminologist asks the prisoner on death row why he was not deterred by legal penalties, is(are) that
    I. it is dangerous for the criminologist
    II. death row inmates have no reason to lie
    III. death row inmates have no reason not to lie
    IV. it begs the question
    V. it ignores those who were deterred
    The CORRECT answer is:

    A. I, III, V   B. I only   C. II, IV, V   D. IV, V
    E. All of the above

47. MOST murderers are people who
    I. never absorbed moral rules as children
    II. are sociopaths
    III. are psychopaths
    IV. became very angry with a loved one
    V. know their victim
    The CORRECT answer is:

    A. I, III, IV   B. I, II, V   C. I only   D. III only   E. IV, V

48. A *major* bone of contention in jurisprudence is the
    I. discretionary powers of judges
    II. lawmaking powers of judges
    III. rigidity of legal decisions
    IV. laxity of lawyers' courtroom maneuvers
    V. techniques used by defense attorneys
    The CORRECT answer is:

    A. I only   B. III only   C. I, II, IV   D. I, III, V   E. III, IV

49. As a general rule, judges differ from criminals in that
    I. the former make more money, on the average
    II. the latter make more money, on the average
    III. judges are more similar to each other than are criminals
    IV. criminals are more similar to each other than are judges
    V. they come from higher social classes
    The CORRECT answer is:

    A. V only   B. I, III, V   C. I, II, III   D. III only   E. III, V

50. One (The) problem(s) besetting the judiciary is(are) *that* 50._____
    I. only lawyers can be judges
    II. judges may be political appointees
    III. judges may be elected officials
    IV. some criminals assassinate judges
    V. there are too few judges
The CORRECT answer is:

A. I, IV, V   B. II, III, V   C. II *only*   D. III *only*   E. IV, V

KEY (CORRECT ANSWERS)

1. D	11. C	21. C	31. D	41. B
2. C	12. E	22. E	32. C	42. E
3. C	13. B	23. D	33. A	43. D
4. D	14. B	24. E	34. E	44. B
5. B	15. D	25. C	35. C	45. E
6. C	16. E	26. A	36. E	46. D
7. B	17. D	27. E	37. D	47. E
8. A	18. D	28. C	38. C	48. A
9. D	19. C	29. C	39. A	49. E
10. C	20. B	30. E	40. E	50. B

EXAMINATION SECTION
TEST 1

DIRECTIONS: Each question or incomplete statement is followed by several suggested answers or completions. Select the one that BEST answers the question or completes the statement. *PRINT THE LETTER OF THE CORRECT ANSWER IN THE SPACE AT THE RIGHT.*

1. Methods of crime control include:
   I. Reformation and treatment
   II. Deterrence
   III. Incapacitation
   IV. Punishment
   V. Educating offenders
   The CORRECT answer is:

   A. I, II   B. I *only*   C. I, II, IV   D. I, III, V
   E. All of the above

   1.____

2. Populations having *no* influence on criminal sentencing are:
   I. Law students
   II. Police
   III. Social workers
   IV. Magistrates
   V. Parole Officers
   The CORRECT answer is:

   A. I *only*   B. II, IV, V   C. I, II, III   D. I, III, IV
   E. None of the above

   2.____

3. The *primary* function of a penal code is to provide a means of
   I. *threatening* our enemies
   II. *modifying* behavior patterns
   III. *eliminating* troublemakers
   IV. *protecting* property
   V. *presenting* a moral example of good behavior
   The CORRECT answer is:

   A. I, IV   B. IV *only*   C. II *only*   D. III, IV
   E. All of the above

   3.____

4. The difference between individual and general crime prevention is that the
   I. *former* can incapacitate individuals
   II. *latter* needs to incapacitate individuals
   III. *latter* emphasizes restraint
   IV. *former* emphasizes deterrence and/or incapacitation
   V. *former* is much more difficult to study
   The CORRECT answer is:

   A. I *only*   B. I, III, V   C. I, III, IV   D. I, II, III, IV
   E. All of the above

   4.____

5. The view that considers social control to be the *primary* function of the law has the following *disadvantages:* It
   I. is indistinguishable from social engineering
   II. leads to fascism
   III. leads to arbitrary rulings
   IV. leads to dogmatism in jurisprudence
   V. lacks public support

   The CORRECT answer is:

   A. I *only* B. II, IV C. III *only* D. I, III, V
   E. I, II, III

6. The evidence shows that criminals *most frequently* consider
   I. their families
   II. costs and benefits
   III. morality
   IV. the law
   V. possible punishment

   The CORRECT answer is:

   A. I *only* B. I, IV C. I, II, V D. II, III, V E. II *only*

7. Norwegian laws against drunk driving tend to prove the criminological theory of
   I. rehabilitationism
   II. retributivism
   III. general prevention
   IV. individual deterrence
   V. lex talones

   The CORRECT answer is:

   A. I, II, V B. I *only* C. III *only* D. II, III, IV
   E. All of the above

8. The famous book(s) on jurisprudence written by H.L.A. Hart is(are):
   I. CRIME AND PUNISHMENT
   II. THE LAW AND SOCIETY
   III. PUNISHMENT AND RESPONSIBILITY
   IV. THE CRIME OF PUNISHMENT
   V. LAW, SOCIETY AND PSYCHOTICS

   The CORRECT answer is:

   A. I *only* B. II *only* C. I, II, V D. III *only* E. III, IV

9. The author of a book advocating rehabilitationism is
   I. H.L.A. Hart
   II. Karl Menninger
   III. Thomas Szasz
   IV. Ivan Illich
   V. Oliver Wendell Holmes

   The CORRECT answer is:

   A. I *only* B. II *only* C. III *only* D. IV *only*
   E. None of the above

10. THE CRIME OF PUNISHMENT was written by
    I. H.L.A. Hart
    II. Karl Menninger
    III. Thomas Szasz
    IV. Ivan Illich
    V. C. Wright Mills
    The CORRECT answer is:

    A. I only   B. II only   C. III only   D. IV only
    E. None of the above

11. CRIME AND PUNISHMENT was a novel that
    I. was written by Dostoevsky
    II. greatly influenced British jurisprudence
    III. was the first influential book on criminal split-personalities
    IV. popularized crime for existentialists
    V. popularized murder in Russia
    The CORRECT answer is:

    A. I only   B. II only   C. I, II, V   D. I, II, III, IV
    E. I, III, IV

12. A *major* influence on modern rehabilitationist theory in criminology was(were) the philosophical school(s) of:
    I. Positivism
    II. Utilitarianism
    III. Deontology
    IV. Existentialism
    V. Natural Law theory
    The CORRECT answer is:

    A. I only   B. II only   C. I, II   D. III, V
    E. All of the above

13. The point(s) historically included in punishment theory is (are):
    I. The work of the Devil
    II. The work of God
    III. Excusing conditions
    IV. Crimes of passion
    V. Psychiatric counseling
    The CORRECT answer is:

    A. I, IV   B. I, II, V   C. I, III   D. IV only   E. III only

14. The thing(s) the law cannot prevent is(are):
    I. Lawbreaking
    II. Lawkeeping
    III. Lawyers
    IV. Judges
    V. Schools
    The CORRECT answer is:

    A. I, III, V   B. I only   C. III only   D. IV, V
    E. All of the above

15. Crimes that CANNOT be prevented include:
    I. Crimes of passion
    II. Civil disobedience
    III. Auto theft
    IV. Drug dealing
    V. Embezzlement
    The CORRECT answer is:

    A. I, II
    B. I, II, III
    C. I, IV, V
    D. IV only
    E. All of the above

16. A person who engages in civil disobedience is one who
    I. is very religious
    II. breaks the law
    III. avoids breaking the law
    IV. acts from passion
    V. acts with premeditation
    The CORRECT answer is:

    A. I, III
    B. I, II, III
    C. II only
    D. III, V
    E. IV, V

17. The thing(s) a civil disobedient must do is(are) to:
    I. Avoid prosecution
    II. Publicize his complaint
    III. Be very conscientious
    IV. Accept legal penalties
    V. Act secretly
    The CORRECT answer is:

    A. I only
    B. II, V
    C. III only
    D. IV only
    E. IV, V

18. The *principal* purpose(s) of entering into civil disobedience is(are) to
    I. prove the sincerity of one's religious beliefs
    II. prove the sincerity of one's political beliefs
    III. change immoral laws
    IV. challenge authoritarian representatives of the law
    V. get publicity
    The CORRECT answer is:

    A. I, IV
    B. I, II, III, IV
    C. II only
    D. III only
    E. III, V

19. The *major* reason(s) that theories of punishment are so important is(are) that:
    I. Being deprived of liberty is harmful
    II. Things that are prima facie wrong need justification
    III. Criminologists need to publish books
    IV. Judges need to refer to academic authorities
    V. Scientific evidence is sufficient to justify punishment
    The CORRECT answer is:

    A. I, II
    B. II only
    C. I, III, V
    D. III, IV, V
    E. None of the above

5 (#1)

20. In criminological theories of punishment, MONTERO'S AIM refers to:
    I. A rehabilitationist theory created by Montero
    II. A retributionist theory created by Montero
    III. The theory advocating protecting criminals from the law
    IV. The theory advocating protecting criminals from the
    V. public
    VI. Unpopular laws
    The CORRECT answer is:

    A. II, III   B. I, IV   C. I only   D. V only   E. IV only

21. The *primary* aim(s) of retributionist theories of punishment is(are) to:
    I. Insure that criminals atone for their wrongs
    II. Encourage would-be criminals to abstain from crime
    III. Deter crime
    IV. Enforce the law
    V. Reform offenders
    The CORRECT answer is:

    A. I only   B. I, II, IV   C. II, III   D. IV, V   E. I, IV

22. The theory called *"retribution in distribution"* advocates that criminals should suffer
    I. in proportion to their crime
    II. to encourage others to desist
    III. but not at all costs
    IV. for their crimes at all costs
    V. penalties identical to those of their victims
    The CORRECT answer is:

    A. I, V   B. II only   C. I, II   D. III only   E. IV only

23. According to *"brute retributivism,"* punishment is
    I. little more than a thirst for revenge
    II. socially satisfying
    III. a crowd pleaser
    IV. a general deterrence
    V. a reforming agent
    The CORRECT answer is:

    A. I only   B. I, II, V   C. I, II, III   D. II, III, IV
    E. III, IV, V

24. The concept(s) *very important* to punishment theory is(are):
    I. Intentions
    II. Passions
    III. Statistics
    IV. Logic
    V. Operant conditioning
    The CORRECT answer is:

    A. I, II   B. I only   C. III only   D. III, IV   E. I, II, V

25. Both rehabilitationists and retributionists can agree that the *outstanding* flaw(s) in the criminal justice system is(are):
    I. Procedural injustice
    II. Influence of criminologists
    III. Patriarchal influences
    IV. Medical intervention
    V. Appeals to higher courts
    The CORRECT answer is:

    A. I only   B. II, III   C. I, III   D. IV only   E. I, II, III

26. Achieving social justice through the criminal law must be balanced against
    I. an oppressive criminal justice system
    II. overly stringent laws
    III. principles of liberty
    IV. due process
    V. rights of privacy
    The CORRECT answer is:

    A. I only   B. I, II, V   C. I, III, IV   D. I, II, III, IV
    E. All of the above

27. The *important* concept(s) that *must* underlie fair judicial decisions include(s):
    I. Precedence
    II. Consistency
    III. Impartiality
    IV. Discretion
    V. Leniency
    The CORRECT answer is:

    A. I only   B. II only   C. I, II, V   D. I, II, III
    E. I, II, IV, V

28. If there is a spurt in crime in a given area, and more police are located there, after which crime rates return to normal, it is *reasonable* to conclude that
    I. the police apprehended the criminals
    II. the police found the cause of the crime
    III. the police presence caused the drop in crime
    IV. the community should increase its police force
    V. detectives participated in the crime resolution
    The CORRECT answer is:

    A. I only   B. I, II   C. I, III   D. III only   E. I, IV

29. Convicted murderers with high recidivism rates *usually* get arrested for
    I. murder
    II. assault
    III. aggravated assault
    IV. auto theft
    V. grand larceny
    The CORRECT answer is:

    A. I only   B. I, II   C. II only   D. III, IV   E. III only

30. A California study of comparative recidivism rates between retributivism and rehabilitationism concluded that
    I. rehabilitation had lower recidivism rates
    II. retributionism had lower recidivism rates
    III. neither recidivism rate was lower than the other
    IV. the study was inconclusive
    V. more rehabilitation programs should be created
    The CORRECT answer is:

    A. I only   B. II only   C. III only   D. IV only
    E. None of the above

31. The factor(s) that appear(s) to increase recidivism is(are):
    I. Keeping people in prison longer
    II. Keeping people in prison more briefly
    III. Refusing to imprison people
    IV. Peer pressure
    V. Temptations to commit crime
    The CORRECT answer is:

    A. I only   B. II only   C. II, III   D. II, IV   E. IV only

32. The improvement(s) that rehabilitation programs achieve over retributivist programs is(are):
    I. They cost less
    II. A higher suicide rate among prisoners
    III. A lower suicide rate among prisoners
    IV. Better relations between inmates and prison staff
    V. They require fewer professionals to implement
    The CORRECT answer is:

    A. I only   B. II, IV   C. III only   D. I, III   E. IV only

33. Dr. Thomas Szasz's MAIN criticism(s) against rehabilitation approaches to punishment is(are) that they
    I. don't work
    II. cost more
    III. treat bad people as sick
    IV. treat sick people as bad
    V. don't use enough professions
    The CORRECT answer is:

    A. I, II   B. IV only   C. III only   D. IV only
    E. II, IV

34. Evidence to date does NOT support the claim(s) that
    I. deterrence is a worthy goal
    II. deterrence is increasing
    III. convicted persons are mentally ill
    IV. convicted persons are sane
    V. prison facilities are inadequate
    The CORRECT answer is:

    A. I, III   B. I, IV   C. II only   D. III only   E. IV only

35. The motive(s) frequently discounted for criminal behavior is(are)
    I. revenge
    II. retaliation
    III. profit
    IV. hostility
    V. necessity
    The CORRECT answer is:

    A. I only   B. II only   C. III,V   D. IV only   E. I, IV

36. A reductivist approach to sentencing recommends that we
    I. increase minimum sentences
    II. decrease lengths of minimum sentences
    III. increase maximum sentences
    IV. decrease maximum sentences
    V. eliminate plea bargaining
    The CORRECT answer is:

    A. I, II   B. II only   C. III only   D. II, IV
    E. None of the above

37. Lengthy sentences are usually the result of
    I. hanging judges
    II. inept lawyers
    III. an increase in serious offenses
    IV. indeterminate sentences
    V. administrative error
    The CORRECT answer is:

    A. I, III   B. II only   C. II, IV   D. IV only.
    E. All of the above

38. The general deterrence approach to punishment and crime prevention works *least well* with respect to
    I. crimes of passion
    II. premeditated crimes
    III. professional criminals
    IV. occasional criminals
    V. white collar crimes
    The CORRECT answer is:

    A. I only   B. II, IV   C. II, III   D. III only
    E. None of the above

39. Methodological difficulties involved in criminological research include :
    I. Determining criteria for success and failure
    II. Adequately classifying population groups
    III. Getting adequate sample populations
    IV. Properly interpreting motivation
    V. Mathematical computations
    The CORRECT answer is:

    A. I, II   B. II, III   C. I, II, III   D. IV only
    E. All of the above

40. In evaluating the long-term effects of punishment upon criminals, one should take into account
    I. constructive uses of leisure
    II. educational enhancement
    III. neighbors' opinions
    IV. attitudinal changes
    V. public reaction to ex-convicts
    The CORRECT answer is:

    A. I, II
    B. III only
    C. I, II, III
    D. I, II, IV
    E. All of the above

41. The significant distinction(s) to make in studies of long-term effects of punishment is(are) between
    I. violent and non-violent crimes
    II. offenders who get caught and the ones who do not
    III. occasional vs. habitual recidivists
    IV. Men and women offenders
    V. Youthful vs. adult offenders
    The CORRECT answer is:

    A. I only
    B. II only
    C. I, III
    D. III only
    E. I, II, IV

42. The disadvantage(s) of being treated for mental illness as opposed to being punished for criminal behavior is(are) that
    I. a diagnosis of the illness is difficult to find
    II. cures are very rare
    III. mental patients don't have the stringent legal protections prisoners have
    IV. it is harder to pick up crime tips
    V. medical personnel agree on prognoses
    The CORRECT answer is:

    A. I, II
    B. I only
    C. III only
    D. I, II, IV
    E. I, III

43. The assumption(s) from the field of psychology that has (have) led some criminologists to become rehabilitationists is(are):
    I. Humans act rationally
    II. Human behavior is the result of antecedent causes
    III. Basic fears motivate humans
    IV. The pleasure principle motivates everyone
    V. Humans act irrationally
    The CORRECT answer is:

    A. I only
    B. II, V
    C. III only
    D. IV only
    E. All of the above

44. Historically, the transition from retributionism to re-habilitationism in crime prevention and treatment corresponds to the
    I. transition from natural law theory to science
    II. rise of capitalism
    III. growth of professional criminals
    IV. changes in public attitudes toward crime
    V. establishment of law in colonial America
    The CORRECT answer is:

    A. I only   B. II only   C. I, II   D. II, III   E. IV only

45. Various roles undertaken by police officers include:
    I. Information gathering
    II. Maintaining order
    III. Enforcing the law
    IV. Serving the public
    V. Counseling victims
    The CORRECT answer is:

    A. I, II   B. II, III, IV, V   C. II, III   D. III, IV
    E. All of the above

46. When police officers maintain order, they usually are
    I. issuing a summons
    II. making an arrest
    III. resolving a dispute
    IV. gathering data for the courts
    V. counseling victims
    The CORRECT answer is:

    A. I only   B. II only   C. I, III   D. III only
    E. All of the above

47. The *majority* of arrests made by police originate from
    I. citizens' complaints
    II. police observation of street incidents
    III. anonymous tip-offs
    IV. underworld informers
    V. computerized records
    The CORRECT answer is:

    A. I only   B. II only   C. II, III   D. I, III, IV
    E. IV only

48. Detectives' contributions to arrest rates can *best* be characterized as:
    I. They make up the largest portion of them
    II. They contribute to approximately 15-20% of them
    III. They barely contribute to arrests at all
    IV. Ancillary
    V. Obstructive
    The CORRECT answer is:

    A. I only   B. II only   C. III only   D. IV only
    E. None of the above

11 (#1)

49. The *most important* group(s) influencing police effectiveness is(are): 49.____
    I. criminals
    II. courts
    III. judges
    IV. citizens
    V. social workers
    The CORRECT answer is:

    A. I *only*   B. II, III   C. III, IV, V   D. IV *only*
    E. All of the above

50. The significant factor(s) in long-term studies of criminal behavior and the effectiveness of 50.____
    punishment is(are):
    I. Whether the criminal's marriage survived
    II. The parole officer's reports
    III. The psychiatric social worker
    IV. Alcoholism
    V. Educational achievement
    The CORRECT answer is:

    A. I *only*   B. I, II   C. II *only*   D. I, II, III
    E. All of the above

KEY (CORRECT ANSWERS)

1. E	11. E	21. E	31. A	41. C
2. E	12. B	22. D	32. E	42. C
3. C	13. E	23. C	33. D	43. B
4. C	14. B	24. B	34. D	44. A
5. A	15. A	25. A	35. C	45. E
6. E	16. D	26. E	36. E	46. D
7. C	17. D	27. D	37. D	47. A
8. D	18. D	28. D	38. A	48. B
9. B	19. A	29. E	39. E	49. D
10. B	20. E	30. C	40. D	50. B

EXAMINATION SECTION
TEST 1

DIRECTIONS: Each question or incomplete statement is followed by several suggested answers or completions. Select the one that BEST answers the question or completes the statement. *PRINT THE LETTER OF THE CORRECT ANSWER IN THE SPACE AT THE RIGHT.*

1. The age group *most* responsible for violent crimes against the person is(are):
    I. 14-18
    II. 18-24
    III. 24-29
    IV. 29-35
    V. 35-45
   The CORRECT answer is:

   A. I *only*
   B. II *only*
   C. III, IV
   D. V *only*
   E. I, II

2. MOST violent crimes are
    I. inter-racial
    II. intra-racial
    III. committed by men
    IV. committed by women
    V. solved by arrest
   The CORRECT answer is:

   A. I *only*
   B. II *only*
   C. I, III
   D. II, V
   E. I, IV

3. Social scientific methods were *first* used to study suicide by the sociologist(s)
    I. H. L. A. Hart
    II. Weber
    III. Durkheim
    IV. Riesman
    V. Oliver Wendell Holmes
   The CORRECT answer is:

   A. I, IV
   B. II, V
   C. III *only*
   D. IV *only*
   E. none of the above

4. Social scientists have shown that deviance is
    I. inherent in certain forms of behavior
    II. conferred upon certain forms of behavior by societies
    III. a normal result of stable institutions
    IV. an abnormal reaction against stable institutions
    V. normal
   The CORRECT answer is:

1. ____

2. ____

3. ____

4. ____

65

A. I only B. II only
C. I, IV D. II, III
E. IV, V

5. Crimes in which there is a *high* probability that the offender and victim were already acquainted with each other include
    I. auto theft
    II. burglary
    III. rape
    IV. murder
    V. embezzlement
The CORRECT answer is:

A. I only B. I, II
C. III, V D. IV only
E. III, IV

6. MOST crimes against the person are committed
    I. at home
    II. near one's place of residence
    III. while traveling in unfamiliar places
    IV. because of alcoholism
    V. on the street
The CORRECT answer is:

A. I, IV B. II only
C. III only D. III, IV
E. IV, V

7. In the United States, the group *most likely* to be victims of crime are
    I. teenagers
    II. women
    III. black men
    IV. black women
    V. children
The CORRECT answer is:

A. I only B. I, II, V
C. II, IV, V D. III, IV
E. III only

8. The country which has the LARGEST proportion of criminal homicides is

A. Canada B. Great Britain
C. United States D. Denmark
E. Sweden

9. According to Interpol, a MAJOR area of crime increase is

A. aggravated assault B. unjustified homicide
C. bribery D. theft
E. none of the above

10. *Ideally,* punishment should be
    I. effective
    II. justified
    III. painless
    IV. inexpensive
    V. discreet
    The CORRECT answer is:

    A. I *only*
    B. I, II
    C. III, IV
    D. III, IV, V
    E. all of the above

11. An increasingly important tool in criminal justice administration is the
    I. psychiatric social worker
    II. intelligence test
    III. personality profile
    IV. cost-benefit analysis
    V. computer
    The CORRECT answer is:

    A. I *only*
    B. I, III
    C. V *only*
    D. IV, V
    E. I, II, III

12. The view holding that human behavior can be scientifically analyzed into causes and effects is called

    A. retributionism
    B. rehabilitationism
    C. psychological determinism
    D. natural law theory
    E. none of the above

13. Both the United States and Canadian legal systems include
    I. writs of assistance
    II. magistrates
    III. traditions from English common law
    IV. the same criminal code
    V. the right of individuals to sue companies
    The CORRECT answer is:

    A. I, II
    B. I, III, V
    C. II *only*
    D. II, III
    E. III, IV, V

14. The U.S. President's Commission on Law Enforcement and the Administration of Justice Task Force reported that
    I. arrest records are incomplete
    II. mathematically, 40% of male U.S. children will be arrested for a non-traffic offense
    III. police and correctional offices have different approaches
    IV. mathematical approaches to crime causation are deficient
    V. crime is clearly decreasing
    The CORRECT answer is:

A. I only B. II, III
C. III, IV D. III, IV, V
E. all of the above

15. The study of *criminal recidivism* includes
    I. penology
    II. sociology
    III. psychology
    IV. jurisprudence
    V. philosophy
    The CORRECT answer is:

    A. I only B. I, II, V
    C. III, IV D. IV only
    E. all of the above

16. *Penology* is the study of
    I. criminals
    II. offenses
    III. prisons
    IV. crime statistics
    V. deviant behavior
    The CORRECT answer is:

    A. I only B. I, II, III, V
    C. III only D. III, IV
    E. all of the above

17. For criminological purposes, a *social problem* is

    A. whatever members of the criminal justice system think it is
    B. a condition which a large number of people believe to be a deviation from a valued norm
    C. any instance in which someone is harmed or hurt
    D. any instance in which there is a financial loss
    E. all of the above

18. The difference between a *subjective* and *objective* social problem, for criminologists, can BEST be characterized as
    I. personal vs. scientific
    II. objective problems are publicly verifiable
    III. problems that are relatively free of controversy are objective
    IV. problems that are idiosyncratic are subjective
    V. quantifiable vs. not quantifiable
    The CORRECT answer is:

    A. I only B. II, III
    C. II, III, IV D. IV only
    E. II, III, IV, V

19. Mass communications have influenced crime in that
   I. televisions are hot items for thieves
   II. people are aware of their relative deprivation
   III. criminals use techniques seen on television to commit crimes
   IV. apprehending criminals is much easier now
   V. criminal behavior has high publicity

   The CORRECT answer is:

   A. I, II
   B. I, III, V
   C. II only
   D. II, III, IV
   E. all of the above

20. According to Weber, power can be characterized as
   I. people realizing their own will against others' resistance
   II. people using extreme means to achieve an end
   III. wanting high prestige and social position
   IV. the achievement of self-sufficiency
   V. economic stability

   The CORRECT answer is:

   A. I only
   B. II only
   C. II, III, IV
   D. III, V
   E. IV only

21. One aspect of crime control and prevention *frequently* emphasized by sociologists is the

   A. influence of drugs and alcohol on crime
   B. class structure of society
   C. probable hidden motives of offenders
   D. total costs to the taxpayer of crime control
   E. none of the above

22. The term *"social norms"* refers to
   I. rules set up by prominent society members
   II. norms of conduct specifying what people ought to do
   III. norms of conduct predicting what people actually do
   IV. behavioral criteria that are normative
   V. statistical profiles of human behavior

   The CORRECT answer is:

   A. I, III, V
   B. II only
   C. II, III
   D. II, IV
   E. IV, V

23. A crucial concept in the social sciences is *"socialization,* which is the process
   I. of training children in a language
   II. of learning to get along with peers
   III. of learning to manipulate society
   IV. children undergo in learning social values
   V. of indoctrination

   The CORRECT answer is:

A. I, II B. I, III, V
C. II *only* D. III, IV, V
E. IV *only*

24. If a law is repealed, the chances are that
    I. it was a bad law
    II. it was an unpopular law
    III. it ceased to reflect people's values
    IV. someone paid for it to be changed
    V. it was unenforceable
    The CORRECT answer is:

    A. I, III B. II *only*
    C. III, V D. IV, V
    E. all of the above

25. Two constitutional guarantees that *frequently* impede the judicial process are those of

    A. freedom of speech and the right to assemble
    B. the right to assemble and due process
    C. due process and the right to a speedy trial
    D. the right to a speedy trial and the right to legal defense
    E. none of the above

26. "Legal paternalism" refers to the view that claims that
    I. the law ought to improve people
    II. laws should respect privacy
    III. laws should restrain people for their own good
    IV. laws should reflect the will of the people
    V. laws regulate social stability
    The CORRECT answer is:

    A. I *only* B. I, III
    C. II *only* D. II, IV, V
    E. III, V

27. The *organic* view of society maintains that
    I. individuals are the basic component of society
    II. groups are the basic component of society
    III. society is in constant flux and change
    IV. society can be quantitatively analyzed
    V. biological causes best account for crime
    The CORRECT answer is:

    A. I *only* B. II *only*
    C. II, III D. III, IV, V
    E. III, V

28. The *atomic* view of society maintains that
    I. individuals are the basic component of society
    II. groups are the basic component of society
    III. society is in constant flux and change
    IV. society can be quantitatively analyzed
    V. various parts of society influence each other
    The CORRECT answer is:

A. I only B. I, IV
C. II only D. II, III, V
E. V only

29. The difference between *ascribed* status and *achieved* status is that the 29.____

    A. former can be falsified
    B. latter can be falsified
    C. former is given, the latter made
    D. former is more valuable than the latter
    E. none of the above

30. Our right to freedom of movement can be outweighed by 30.____
    I. having smallpox
    II. committing a crime
    III. others' right to the same
    IV. laws against vagrancy
    V. endangering others
    The CORRECT answer is:

    A. I, II B. I, II, III
    C. III, IV D. III, IV, V
    E. all of the above

31. The Prohibition Laws of the 20's and 30's are an example of 31.____
    I. ineffective legislation
    II. paternalistic law
    III. retributionism
    IV. general prevention
    V. positivism
    The CORRECT answer is:

    A. I only B. I, II, V
    C. II only D. III, IV
    E. III, IV, V

32. One factor heavily influencing criminology theories is 32.____
    I. ideology
    II. academic institutions
    III. quantitative methods
    IV. moral beliefs
    V. scientific verification
    The CORRECT answer is:

    A. I only B. I, II
    C. I, IV D. II, III, IV
    E. V only

33. The concept of "overcriminalization" refers to the view that criminals 33.____

    A. are genetically deviant
    B. know right from wrong
    C. are perfectable
    D. are harassed by legal procedure
    E. commit too many crimes

34. Representatives of the criminal justice system came under attack after the 1960's because
    I. many people considered the law unresponsive
    II. people began to complain of courtroom delays and racism
    III. the law was perceived to protect only the wealthy
    IV. the police hated hippies
    V. they had bad publicity
    The CORRECT answer is:

    A. I only
    B. I, II, III
    C. II only
    D. III, IV
    E. IV, V

35. Criminological research focuses upon
    I. kinds of people
    II. kinds of environment
    III. power and conflict
    IV. kinds of laws
    V. subliminal motivation
    The CORRECT answer is:

    A. I only
    B. I, II
    C. I, II, III
    D. II, IV, V
    E. III, IV, V

36. *Positivism* seriously influenced criminology in that it
    I. denied free will
    II. separated morality from law
    III. rejected negative thinking
    IV. considered science as a model
    V. invalidated previous models
    The CORRECT answer is:

    A. I only
    B. I, II, IV
    C. III only
    D. IV, V
    E. all of the above

37. The origin of prison work-houses is attributable to
    I. the results of cost-benefit analyses
    II. the Protestant work ethic
    III. the belief that hard work is morally edifying
    IV. the desire to see criminals suffer
    V. philanthropic efforts
    The CORRECT answer is:

    A. I only
    B. I, IV, V
    C. II only
    D. II, III, IV
    E. all of the above

38. The "medical model" of criminology assumes that
    I. doctors know more about people than lawyers
    II. crime is an illness that can be cured
    III. there are biological causes for criminal behavior
    IV. crime is NOT a social reaction to the environment
    V. people make rational decisions
    The CORRECT answer is:

    A. I only
    B. I, III
    C. II, III
    D. II, III, IV
    E. III, IV, V

39. The "environmental model" of criminology assumes that
    I. environmental factors can cause crime
    II. people adapt to environments to survive
    III. crime can be socially adaptive
    IV. individual therapy can be an effective crime deterrent
    V. biological factors contribute to criminal behavior
    The CORRECT answer is:

    A. I only
    B. I, II
    C. I, II, III
    D. II, IV, V
    E. all of the above

40. Environmental criminologists believe that
    I. only individuals can be pathological
    II. societies can be pathological
    III. criminal behavior is rational
    IV. criminal behavior is irrational
    V. psychological analysis is crucial
    The CORRECT answer is:

    A. I only
    B. I, IV, V
    C. II only
    D. II, III
    E. III, V

41. "Mens rea" refers to
    I. male offenders
    II. mental items
    III. motives
    IV. passion and premeditation
    V. cyclical activities
    The CORRECT answer is:

    A. I only
    B. II only
    C. II, III, IV
    D. II, III, V
    E. II only

42. The reason we do NOT perform public drawing and quartering of mass murderers is that it

    A. is very sloppy
    B. would provide people with gruesome pleasure
    C. is cruel and inhumane punishment

D. is cruel and unusual punishment
E. all of the above

43. MOST criminologists view the state as
    I. the source of all problems in law enforcement
    II. the source of law
    III. a neutral entity with respect to crime
    IV. largely uninvolved with the criminal justice system
    V. unavoidable and unfortunate
    The CORRECT answer is:

    A. I, IV, V   B. II only
    C. II, III, V   D. III only
    E. III, IV

44. Recent criminology theory views the state as
    I. a nuisance
    II. the source of law
    III. politically involved with criminal justice administration
    IV. a non-neutral power
    V. a neutral power
    The CORRECT answer is:

    A. I, V   B. II only
    C. II, III, V   D. III only
    E. III, IV

45. A topic much discussed in the history of philosophy and of relevance to criminology is that of
    I. psychological determinism
    II. free will and determinism
    III. morality and the law
    IV. paternalism
    V. pathology
    The CORRECT answer is:

    A. I, IV   B. II only
    C. II, IV   D. III, V
    E. all of the above

46. One factor difficult for criminologists to evaluate is
    I. motives
    II. intentions
    III. the purpose of the law
    IV. court procedures
    V. prison statistics
    The CORRECT answer is:

    A. I only   B. I, II
    C. III only   D. III, IV, V
    E. IV, V

47. A 19th century theory of criminology was

   A. positivism
   B. natural law
   C. phrenology
   D. cybernetics
   E. none of the above

48. The study of *phrenology* concerned
   I. biological Darwinism
   II. head shapes
   III. genes
   IV. environmental influences
   V. behavior modification

   The CORRECT answer is:

   A. I *only*
   B. I, II, III
   C. II *only*
   D. II, III, V
   E. IV, V

49. The *primary* contention of phrenologists was that

   A. only those who adapted, perhaps using crime, survived
   B. head shape determines the functions of one's brain
   C. criminal behavior is built into our genetic code
   D. environments influence criminals more than anything else
   E. none of the above

50. Geneticists in criminology claim that

   A. head shapes determine brain functions
   B. environments shape criminal behavior
   C. chromosomes determine violent behavior
   D. humans have free will
   E. all of the above

KEY (CORRECT ANSWERS)

1.	B	11.	D	21.	B	31.	C	41.	C
2.	C	12.	C	22.	D	32.	C	42.	D
3.	C	13.	D	23.	E	33.	C	43.	E
4.	D	14.	E	24.	C	34.	B	44.	E
5.	E	15.	A	25.	C	35.	C	45.	C
6.	B	16.	C	26.	B	36.	B	46.	B
7.	D	17.	B	27.	C	37.	C	47.	C
8.	C	18.	E	28.	B	38.	D	48.	C
9.	D	19.	D	29.	C	39.	C	49.	B
10.	B	20.	A	30.	E	40.	D	50.	D

EXAMINATION SECTION
TEST 1

DIRECTIONS: Each question or incomplete statement is followed by several suggested answers or completions. Select the one that BEST answers the question or completes the statement. *PRINT THE LETTER OF THE CORRECT ANSWER IN THE SPACE AT THE RIGHT.*

1. The concept of "conscience" is important in the criminological theories of
    I. positivism
    II. phrenology
    III. natural law
    IV. environmentalism
    V. rehabilitationism
   The CORRECT answer is:

   A. I, III, IV B. II, V
   C. I, II, III D. III only
   E. none of the above

   1._____

Questions 2-4.

DIRECTIONS: Questions 2 to 4 refer to the following theories:
   Theory A: Individuals calculate pains and pleasures of crime and pursue that which brings pleasure.
   Theory B: Criminals have distinctive body types compared with non-criminals.
   Theory C: Social processes cause criminal behavior.

2. The criminological theory described in Theory A is

   A. classical theory B. biological positivism
   C. sociological determinism D. natural law theory
   E. behavior modification

   2._____

3. The criminological theory described in Theory B is

   A. classical theory B. biological positivism
   C. sociological determinism D. natural law theory
   E. behavior modification

   3._____

4. The criminological theory described in Theory C is

   A. classical theory B. biological positivism
   C. sociological determinism D. natural law theory
   E. behavior modification

   4._____

5. The theory claiming that individuals have free choice is
    I. classical theory
    II. biological positivism
    III. sociological determinism
    IV. natural law theory
    V. behavior modification
   The CORRECT answer is:

   5._____

A. I, IV B. II only
C. III, IV, V D. IV only
E. IV, V

6. The theory claiming that individuals MUST act as they do is

   A. classical theory B. biological positivism
   C. sociological determinism D. natural law theory
   E. behavior modification

7. The concept of "overreach" in criminal law refers to
   I. using law to regulate private moral conduct
   II. law enforcement officers stretching legal procedures
   III. invasion of privacy by law enforcement officers
   IV. excessive legislation
   V. excessive use of psychiatric social workers in courts
   The CORRECT answer is:

   A. I only B. II only
   C. II, III D. III, IV
   E. V only

8. Problems caused by "overreach" are that it
   I. increases the cost of criminal activity
   II. depletes law enforcement resources
   III. concerns victimless crimes
   IV. violates individual autonomy
   V. costs too much
   The CORRECT answer is:

   A. I, III, IV B. II, III, V
   C. II, IV, V D. III, IV
   E. all of the above

9. The view that "crime is the unanticipated outcome of social institutions that thwart people in their effort to acquire the very goods society encourages them to pursue" is

   A. positivism B. determinism
   C. anomie D. environmentalism
   E. dissociation

10. The author of SOCIAL STRUCTURE AND ANOMIE was

    A. Emile Durkheim B. R. K. Merton
    C. C. Wright Mills D. George Herbert Mead
    E. Oliver Wendell Holmes

11. The author of ASPECTS OF ETHNOMETHODOLOGY was

    A. Emile Durkheim B. R. K. Merton
    C. C. Wright Mills D. George Herbert Mead
    E. Oliver Wendell Holmes

12. The author of SUICIDE: A STUDY IN SOCIOLOGY was

    A. Emile Durkheim B. R. K. Merton
    C. C. Wright Mills D. George Herbert Mead
    E. Oliver Wendell Holmes

13. The author of THE DIVISION OF LABOUR IN SOCIETY was

    A. Emile Durkheim
    B. R. K. Merton
    C. C. Wright Mills
    D. George Herbert Mead
    E. Karl Marx

14. The author of THE POWER ELITE was

    A. Emile Durkheim
    B. R. K. Merton
    C. C. Wright Mills
    D. George Herbert Mead
    E. Karl Marx

15. The author of THE PSYCHOLOGY OF PUNITIVE JUSTICE was

    A. Emile Durkheim
    B. R. K. Merton
    C. C. Wright Mills
    D. George Herbert Mead
    E. Oliver Wendell Holmes

16. The view that the rights of individuals ought to be protected against social institutions is central to the criminological school of

    A. classicism
    B. positivism
    C. retributionism
    D. determinism
    E. rehabilitationism

17. A *frequent* assumption of criminological theory is that crime
    I. is ubiquitous
    II. is a male, working-class activity
    III. is a female, middle-class activity
    IV. should be completely abolished
    V. does not pay

    The CORRECT answer is:

    A. I, III, V
    B. II *only*
    C. II, IV, V
    D. III, IV
    E. all of the above

18. Cesare Lombroso's theory of *atavism* claimed that

    A. extreme criminal behavior causes autism
    B. crime is a result of dysfunctional behavior
    C. criminals are reversions to primitive man
    D. parapsychology can help detectives find criminals
    E. crime is caused by positive reinforcement

19. According to one theory, the chromosomal arrangement that causes the individual to commit crimes is

    A. XX   B. XY   C. XXY   D. XYY   E. YYY

20. The view that criminals choose pleasurable activities over painful ones is reminiscent of the philosophical school of

    A. Kantianism
    B. natural law theory
    C. utilitarianism
    D. contract theory
    E. humanism

21. The claim that, criminal behavior can be cured by operant conditioning is attributable to the psychological school of

    A. cognitive psychology
    B. humanist psychology
    C. behavior modification
    D. Freudian psychoanalysis
    E. humanism

22. One feature of the criminal justice system without which it could NOT exist is

    A. files
    B. computers
    C. coercion
    D. weapons
    E. toleration

23. The concept of *collective conscience* is attributable to

    A. C. Wright Mills
    B. Durkheim
    C. G. H. Mead
    D. Bentham
    E. Carl Jung

24. Weber's concept of *moral pragmatism* claims that

    A. morality and the law are separate entities
    B. morality is irrelevant in evaluating crime
    C. policies on crime are justified by certain values
    D. policies on crime ought to be pluralistic
    E. several policies on crime can be equally valid

25. The phenomenon of *value generalisation* refers to

    A. people being socialized into particular norms
    B. general norms rather than specific ones being emphasized
    C. increasing specialized tasks in society
    D. decreasing specialized tasks in society
    E. someone projecting his norms onto others

26. The result of value generalization for criminology is that

    A. predatory acts will be increasingly criminalized
    B. nonpredatory acts will be increasingly criminalized
    C. nonpredatory acts will be decreasingly criminalized
    D. predatory acts will be decreasingly criminalized
    E. predation will cease to be a factor in criminology

27. A prominent critic of medieval European justice was

    A. Machiavelli
    B. Beccaria
    C. Bentham
    D. Durkheim
    E. Marx

28. During the 18th and 19th centuries, one result of classical criminological theory was
    I. an increase in crimes punishable by the death penalty
    II. a decrease in crimes punishable by the death penalty
    III. fewer innocent people being punished
    IV. more innocent people being punished
    V. more law schools

    The CORRECT answer is:

A. I B. II
C. II, IV D. III, V
E. IV, V

29. The author of COMMENTARIES ON THE LAWS OF ENGLAND is

    A. Jeremy Bentham B. C. Wright Mills
    C. William Blackstone D. Oliver Wendell Holmes
    E. none of the above

30. A concept originating in Roman law and affecting American criminal legislation based on English common law is

    A. nonage B. tort
    C. death penalty D. discretion
    E. probation

31. The old legal principle of *nonage* refers to
    I. exempting children from legal responsibility
    II. exempting insane people from legal responsibility
    III. establishing legal limits for liability
    IV. people under age seven
    V. equality before the courts
    The CORRECT answer is:

    A. I, IV B. II *only*
    C. II, III, V D. III, IV
    E. IV, V

32. The proportion of defendants *successfully* pleading insanity before 1954 was *approximately*

    A. 0.2% B. 2% C. 5% D. 20% E. 30%

33. The proportion of defendants pleading insanity *after* 1955 was *approximately*

    A. 0.2% B. 2% C. 5% D. 10% E. 20%

34. One feature of American law that was NOT inherited from British common law is

    A. nonage B. statute of limitations
    C. insanity defense D. negligence
    E. mitigating excuses

35. The *statute of limitations* refers to crimes
    I. committed 20 or more years ago
    II. no one remembers
    III. not prosecuted within a legal time limit
    IV. not prosecuted speedily
    V. that harm no one
    The CORRECT answer is:

    A. I, II, IV B. II, III
    C. II, III, IV D. III *only*
    E. IV, V

36. Crimes *exempted* from the statutes of limitations include
    I. robbery

II. murder
III. treason
IV. forgery
V. assault

The CORRECT answer is:

A. I, II, V
B. II only
C. II, III, IV
D. III, IV
E. none of the above

37. One factor that can *falsely* indicate an increase in crime is
    I. inflation
    II. ineptness
    III. sloppy recordkeeping
    IV. corrupt police
    V. false witnesses

    The CORRECT answer is:

    A. I only
    B. II only
    C. II, III, V
    D. II, IV, V
    E. IV only

38. The view that slums are high crime areas
    I. came about from prejudice and racism
    II. is based on well-established police statistics
    III. is based on the fact that police are called there most often
    IV. assumes that victims generally report crimes
    V. proves that anomie causes crime

    The CORRECT answer is:

    A. I, II, IV
    B. II, III, V
    C. III only
    D. III, IV
    E. all of the above

39. Suicide is
    I. illegal
    II. legal
    III. immoral
    IV. a definite sign of mental illness
    V. common in the United States

    The CORRECT answer is:

    A. I, IV
    B. II only
    C. III, IV, V
    D. IV only
    E. IV, V

40. In its consideration of the penalties to be imposed for drug offenses, the President's Commission on Law Enforcement and Administration of Justice has recommended that

    A. suspended sentences, probation, and parole be prohibited for all but the first offense of unlawful possession
    B. the policy of mandatory minimum terms of imprisonment be maintained
    C. maximum sentences for possession with intent to sell be made more severe

D. courts and correctional authorities be given enough discretion to deal flexibly with violators
E. plea bargaining not be used in cases involving drug trafficking

41. In a field study, two police forces were compared in their handling of juvenile delinquents. The first force put particular emphasis on education, training, merit promotions, and centralized control. The second force relied more on organization by precinct, seniority, and on-the-job experience. In regard to the rates of processing (police contacts short of arrest but requiring an official record) and arrest (formal police action against the juvenile), it was found that

    A. the processing rate for the first force was higher, but the arrest rate was lower
    B. the arrest rate for the first force was higher, but the processing rate was lower
    C. both the processing rate and the arrest rate were significantly higher for the first force
    D. both the processing rate and the arrest rate were significantly lower for the first force
    E. no conclusion could be drawn relating the arrest and processing rate

42. The President's Commission on Law Enforcement and Administration of Justice has recommended that undergraduate programs for potential and existing law enforcement personnel emphasize

    A. vocational subjects   B. liberal arts
    C. management principles   D. technical courses
    E. business courses

43. In its survey on the capability of selected police departments to control civil disorders, the National Advisory Commission on Civil Disorders found that the MOST critical deficiency of all was inadequacy of

    A. training programs   B. mobilization planning
    C. logistical support   D. intelligence gathering
    E. public policy

44. Following are four statements concerning the rights of defendants in criminal proceedings.
    1. Before the police begin to question a suspect, he must be informed of his rights to remain silent and to be represented by a lawyer.
    2. The right to counsel and the guarantee against self-incrimination have been extended to defendants appearing in state criminal courts.
    3. Questioning of a suspect in custody is prohibited unless counsel is present.
    4. When an investigation shifts to the accusatory stage, a defendant is entitled to counsel, even during interrogation before indictment.
    Which of the following choices lists ALL of the above statements that are true?

    A. 1, 2, 3 and 4   B. 1, 2 and 4, but not 3
    C. 2, 3 and 4, but not 1   D. 2 and 4, but not 1 and 3
    E. 1, 2 and 3 but not 4

45. In the context of civil disorder, appearances and reality are of almost equal importance in the handling of citizen complaints against the police.
Which one of the following is MOST consistent with the viewpoint of the foregoing statement?

A. The police should not be the only municipal agency subject to outside scrutiny and review.
B. The benefits and liabilities of civilian review boards nave both been exaggerated
C. The police department itself should receive and act on complaints in order to protect police against unfounded charges.
D. In addition to adequate machinery for handling complaints, there must be belief among citizens that the procedures are adequate
E. The police should only have to answer charges made by responsible citizens.

46. Suppose that, at a police training lecture, you are told that many of the men in our penal institutions today are second and third offenders. Of the following, the most valid inference you can make SOLELY on the basis of this statement is that

    A. second offenders are not easily apprehended
    B. patterns of human behavior are not easily changed
    C. modern laws are not sufficiently flexible
    D. laws do not breed crimes
    E. crime is a way of life for most inmates

47. The President's Commission on Law Enforcement and Administration of Justice obtained data from various sources on the victims of crime. This data shows some very interesting relationships which may very well have nationwide application.
Based on this data, which ONE of the following statements concerning the victims of violent crimes against the person is LEAST likely to be accurate?

    A. A male is most likely to be a victim in a major crime against the person (except homicide) when he is on the street.
    B. The highest victimization rate for robbery is for males between the ages of 20 and 29.
    C. A female is most likely to be a victim in a major crime against the person (except homicide) when she is in her place of residence.
    D. An assaultive crime against a white victim is more likely to be committed by a black male than a white male.
    E. A very high percentage of the victims of assaults, rapes, and homicides are acquainted with the perpetrator of the crime.

Questions 48-50.

DIRECTIONS: Questions 48 to 50 are to be answered SOLELY on the basis of the following passage.

The criminal justice system is generally regarded as having the basic objective of reducing crime. However, one must also consider its larger objective of minimizing the total social costs associated with crime and crime control. Both of these components are complex and difficult to measure completely. The social costs associated with crime come from the long- and short-term physical damage, psychological harm, and property losses to victims as a result of crimes committed. Crime also creates serious indirect effects. It can induce a feeling of insecurity that is only partially reflected in business losses and economic disruption due to anxiety about venturing into high-crime-rate areas.

Balanced against these costs associated with crime must be the consequences of actions taken to reduce them. Money spent on developing, maintaining, and operating criminal justice agencies is part of the cost of the crime control system. But there are also indirect costs, such as welfare payments to prisoners' families, income lost by offenders who are denied good jobs, legal fees, and wages lost by witnesses. In addition, there are penalties suffered by suspects erroneously arrested or sentenced, the limitation on personal liberty resulting from police surveillance, and the invasion of privacy in maintaining criminal records.

48. Of the following, the MOST appropriate title for this passage would be

    A. The Effectiveness of Crime Control Efforts
    B. Protecting Citizens' Rights
    C. The Costs of Crime
    D. Improving the Criminal Justice System
    E. Is Justice Worth the Cost?

49. According to this passage, all of the following are indirect costs of the crime control system EXCEPT

    A. wages lost by witnesses
    B. money spent for legal services
    C. payments made to the families of prisoners
    D. money spent on operating criminal justice agencies
    E. income lost by offenders who are denied good jobs

50. According to this passage, actions taken to reduce crime

    A. will reduce the indirect costs of the crime control system
    B. may result in a decrease of personal liberty
    C. may cause psychological harm to victims of crime
    D. should immediately start improving the criminal justice system
    E. may cost more than the potential crimes it prevents

KEY (CORRECT ANSWERS)

1. D	11. B	21. C	31. A	41. C
2. A	12. A	22. C	32. A	42. B
3. B	13. A	23. C	33. B	43. A
4. C	14. C	24. D	34. B	44. B
5. A	15. D	25. B	35. D	45. D
6. C	16. E	26. C	36. C	46. B
7. A	17. B	27. B	37. A	47. D
8. E	18. C	28. B	38. D	48. C
9. C	19. D	29. C	39. B	49. D
10. B	20. C	30. A	40. D	50. B

EXAMINATION SECTION
TEST 1

DIRECTIONS: Each question or incomplete statement is followed by several suggested answers or completions. Select the one that BEST answers the question or completes the statement. *PRINT THE LETTER OF THE CORRECT ANSWER IN THE SPACE AT THE RIGHT.*

1. A *necessary* component of predatory crime is
    I. physical harm done to the victim
    II. mens rea
    III. intent to harm on the part of the offender
    IV. a victim
    V. negligence
   The CORRECT answer is:

   A. I *only*
   B. I, II, V
   C. II *only*
   D. II, III, IV
   E. III, V

   1._____

2. The literal translation of the Latin "mens rea" is

   A. guilty conscience
   B. intention
   C. motive
   D. evil mind
   E. negligence

   2._____

3. Robbery DIFFERS from burglary in that the
    I. former involves a victim
    II. latter involves coercion
    III. former involves coercion
    IV. former involves a weapon
    V. former always involves personal injury
   The CORRECT answer is:

   A. I *only*
   B. I, II
   C. I, III
   D. IV, V
   E. V *only*

   3._____

4. Statistics on the crime rate in New York City
    I. bear out the popular image that it is very bad
    II. do not bear out the popular image that it is very bad
    III. show that it is in the top five most crime-ridden cities
    IV. show that it is much safer than people think
    V. prove that overcrowding causes crime
   The CORRECT answer is:

   A. I *only*
   B. I, III
   C. II *only*
   D. II, IV
   E. V *only*

   4._____

5. One supplement to police records useful to estimate crime frequency is

   A. interviews with victims
   B. interviews with convicted criminals
   C. victim surveys

   5._____

87

D. FBI statistics
E. Labor Department statistics

6. The LARGEST differentiations by sex of offenders are seen in crimes such as
   I. theft
   II. assault
   III. disorderly conduct
   IV. burglary
   V. embezzlement
   The CORRECT answer is:

   A. I only
   B. II, III
   C. II, IV
   D. IV, V
   E. V only

7. Crimes committed by men are, for the most part,
   I. malicious mischief
   II. burglary
   III. concealed weapons
   IV. assault
   V. shoplifting
   The CORRECT answer is:

   A. I only
   B. I, II, V
   C. II, III
   D. II, III, IV
   E. IV only

8. Crimes *most likely* NOT to be reported to the police include
   I. forgery
   II. rape
   III. theft
   IV. burglary
   V. incest
   The CORRECT answer is:

   A. I, II, V
   B. II only
   C. II, III
   D. IV only
   E. III, IV, V

9. The crimes *most likely* to be committed WITHOUT the criminal being arrested are
   I. burglary
   II. assault
   III. murder
   IV. theft
   V. robbery
   The CORRECT answer is:

   A. I, IV
   B. II, III
   C. II, III, IV
   D. III, V
   E. IV, V

10. A concept crucial in apprehending suspects for such crimes as assault and rape is

    A. mens rea
    B. actus reus
    C. modus operandi
    D. corpus delecti
    E. lex talisnis

11. Crimes *generally* committed by teenagers are
    I. done to gain money
    II. more violent than those by adults
    III. largely deterred by the threat of incarceration
    IV. performed to demonstrate skills
    V. bank robbery

    The CORRECT answer is:

    A. I *only*
    B. II, IV
    C. III, IV, V
    D. III, V
    E. IV *only*

12. Suspects who were bound and thrown into a river were
    I. said to have a "trial by ordeal"
    II. subjected to the Inquisition
    III. innocent if they drowned
    IV. going to be killed no matter what
    V. usually found innocent

    The CORRECT answer is:

    A. I *only*
    B. I, III, IV
    C. II, III
    D. IV *only*
    E. III, V

13. The *labeling theory* in criminology claims that

    A. sociologists should avoid labeling criminals
    B. criminals act so as to portray their label
    C. it is unfair to stereotype individuals
    D. Freud's theory about early childhood is correct
    E. early childhood experiences influence criminal behavior

14. A Freudian explanation of crime causation would claim that
    I. the offender's superego failed to control his id
    II. the offender's ego was artificially suppressed
    III. repressive desublimation causes crime
    IV. lack of mother-love contributed to the crime
    V. negative reinforcement in external stimuli caused criminal behavior

    The CORRECT answer is:

    A. I *only*
    B. II *only*
    C. II, III, V
    D. III, IV
    E. all of the above

15. The contemporary criminologist and psychologist Eysenck claims that

    A. psychoanalytic theory could help reform criminals
    B. mesomorphs are typical criminal types

C. mesomorphs are not typical criminal types
D. ectomorphs are typical criminal types
E. there are more mesomorphs than endomorphs

16. The Q theory that an extra Y chromosome causes criminal behavior
    I. has been shown to be founded
    II. has been shown to be unfounded
    III. was based on statistical fallacies
    IV. has yet to be proven or disproven
    V. simplifies criminologist research
    The CORRECT answer is:

    A. I only
    B. I, V
    C. II only
    D. II, III
    E. IV, V

17. The peak crime rate occurring in adolescence is caused by
    I. the length and ambiguity of adolescence
    II. the probability that adolescents like energetic activity
    III. isolating adolescents from other age groups
    IV. a lack of formal groups for adolescents
    V. lack of parental guidance
    The CORRECT answer is:

    A. V only
    B. II only
    C. III only
    D. III, IV, V
    E. I, III, IV

18. Violent crimes, when compared with early American history, prove to be
    I. hard to explain
    II. compatible with our history
    III. a natural offshoot of American history
    IV. on the increase
    V. an anomaly
    The CORRECT answer is:

    A. I only
    B. I, II, IV, V
    C. II only
    D. II, III
    E. III, IV, V

19. Under the law, homicide is
    I. always wrong or illegal
    II. sometimes excused
    III. sometimes justified
    IV. committed whether it was intended or not
    V. punishable by death
    The CORRECT answer is:

    A. I only
    B. II, III
    C. II, III, IV
    D. II, V
    E. IV, V

20. The American region that has the HIGHEST homicide rate is the   20.____

    A. Northeast   B. Southeast
    C. Southwest   D. Northwest
    E. Midwest

21. The 1914 Harrison Act   21.____

    A. outlawed adultery
    B. decriminalized prostitution
    C. criminalized heroin and cocaine
    D. decriminalized gambling
    E. decriminalized marijuana

22. The Eighteenth Amendment to the Constitution   22.____

    A. decriminalized alcohol consumption
    B. outlawed alcohol consumption
    C. gave women the vote
    D. made slavery illegal
    E. legalized interstate commerce

23. The Pinkerton detectives   23.____
        I. were created by railroad magnates
        II. were designed to stop outlaws like Jesse James and Billy the Kid
        III. rarely got their man
        IV. most often did get their man
        V. were carefully trained in crime control techniques
    The CORRECT answer is:

    A. I *only*   B. I, II, V
    C. I, III   D. II, III
    E. II, IV, V

24. The UNIFORM CRIME REPORTS are   24.____
        I. based on fallacious statistics
        II. published yearly
        III. publish semi-annually
        IV. by the FBI
        V. not uniform
    The CORRECT answer is:

    A. I, V   B. I, II
    C. II *only*   D. II, III, V
    E. II, IV

25. MOST statistical information for the UNIFORM CRIME REPORT comes from   25.____
        I. citizen surveys
        II. citizen reports
        III. police reports
        IV. court data
        V. prison interviews
    The CORRECT answer is:

6 (#1)

    A. I only
    B. II only
    C. II, III
    D. III only
    E. IV, V

26. Fear of crime *most particularly* affects
    I. youths
    II. the elderly
    III. women
    IV. blacks
    V. men
    The CORRECT answer is:

    A. I only
    B. I, II, V
    C. II only
    D. II, III, IV
    E. III, V

27. People MOST fearful of crime in the home are
    A. those living in big cities
    B. those living in small towns
    C. elderly men
    D. those who have already been victimized
    E. none of the above

28. In its "crime index offenses," the FBI includes
    A. the most frequent crimes
    B. the most serious crimes
    C. minor crimes which are on the rise
    D. significant white collar crimes
    E. every crime committed

29. Crimes in the "crime index offenses" category include
    I. criminal homicide, rape
    II. assault, robbery
    III. burglary, larceny
    IV. auto theft
    V. embezzlement
    The CORRECT answer is:

    A. I only
    B. I, II, IV, V
    C. II, III, IV
    D. III only
    E. all of the above

30. The *approximate* rate of increase in crimes included in the "crime index offenses" category between 1968-1977 was

    A. 5-10%
    B. 10-15%
    C. 15-20%
    D. 20-35%
    E. 50%

31. In any given year, there are ALWAYS MORE
    I. crimes of violence than of property
    II. crimes of property than of violence
    III. crimes in cities than rural areas
    IV. victims than offenders
    V. criminals than victims
    The CORRECT answer is:

    A. I only
    B. II only
    C. II, III
    D. III, IV
    E. V only

32. Among the weaknesses in UNIFORM CRIME REPORTS statistics are a(n)
    I. absence of data from some police departments
    II. over-reporting from rural areas
    III. over-reporting from urban areas
    IV. under-reporting from the South
    V. lack of accessibility
    The CORRECT answer is:

    A. I only
    B. I, II, IV
    C. I, III
    D. IV, V
    E. none of the above

33. A subtler problem in the accuracy of UNIFORM CRIME REPORT data is that of
    I. interpreting diverse statistics
    II. detecting computer miscalculations
    III. consistent classification
    IV. meaningful commentary
    V. excluding significant crimes
    The CORRECT answer is:

    A. I only
    B. II, IV
    C. III only
    D. II, III, V
    E. all of the above

34. An important source of data about juvenile delinquency is

    A. parents' reports to police
    B. school records
    C. police records
    D. juvenile court records
    E. childhood experiences

35. Juvenile delinquency increased *approximately* 5% between 1974 and 1975. This is *particularly* important because
    I. adolescents are more affluent than ever
    II. the adolescent population was up 3%
    III. the adolescent population was down 1%
    IV. crimes of juvenile delinquency are more brutal
    V. American youth culture serves as a role model for the world
    The CORRECT answer is:

A. I only
B. I, II, IV
C. III only
D. III, IV, V
E. IV only

36. During 1968-1977, arrests of persons under 18 for major violent crimes

    A. decreased 1%
    B. increased 5%
    C. increased 35%
    D. increased 45%
    E. increased 60%

37. The Juvenile Justice Standards Commission is made up of
    I. parents and lawyers
    II. psychiatrists and sociologists
    III. judges
    IV. penologists
    V. juveniles

    The CORRECT answer is:

    A. I only
    B. II, IV, V
    C. III, IV
    D. III, IV, V
    E. all of the above

38. The Juvenile Justice Standards Commission, after studying the problem of juvenile delinquency, recommended that
    I. youths 14 and up should be prosecuted as adults
    II. youths 16 and 17 should be prosecuted as adults
    III. only youths committing violent crimes should be treated as adults
    IV. all youths committing frequent crimes should be treated as adults
    V. parents resort to old-fashioned discipline

    The CORRECT answer is:

    A. I only
    B. I, III, V
    C. II only
    D. II, III
    E. IV only

39. Another recommendation of the Juvenile Justice Standards Commission was that juveniles should
    I. be reformed by social scientists
    II. be prosecuted by lawyers
    III. be processed in civil-court environments
    IV. be processed in criminal-court environments
    V. NOT be prosecuted at all

    The CORRECT answer is:

    A. I only
    B. I, III
    C. II only
    D. II, IV
    E. V only

40. One crime recommended for lenient handling by the Juvenile Justice Standards Commission is

    A. shoplifting
    B. vandalism
    C. running away from home
    D. assault
    E. sexual assault

41. The *approximate* percentage of crimes cleared by arrest in a given year is   41.____

    A. 10%   B. 20%   C. 50%   D. 60%   E. 70%

42. Generally speaking, crimes cleared by arrest are MOST often   42.____

    A. crimes reported by family members
    B. bank robbery and similar crimes
    C. crimes of property rather than crimes against the person
    D. crimes against the person rather than crimes of property
    E. white collar crimes

43. Overall, arrest data is MOST informative about   43.____

    A. crimes   B. criminals
    C. police activities   D. social instability
    E. subculture behavior patterns

44. Persons under 25 years of age account for *approximately* _____ of crime.   44.____

    A. 10%   B. 20%   C. 30%   D. 40%   E. 50%

45. Youth crime, according to the statistics, appears to be   45.____
    I. increasing in major cities
    II. increasing in suburbs
    III. focused on gang members
    IV. focused on ordinary citizens
    V. decreasing gradually
    The CORRECT answer is:

    A. I, IV   B. II *only*
    C. II, III   D. III, V
    E. V *only*

46. According to statistics, MOST persons arrested for crimes   46.____
    I. are guilty
    II. are innocent
    III. have committed other crimes
    IV. are male
    V. are caught in the act
    The CORRECT answer is:

    A. I *only*   B. I, III
    C. II, IV   D. III, IV, V
    E. IV *only*

47. Males are arrested *approximately* _____ times as often as females.   47.____

    A. two   B. three
    C. five   D. ten
    E. twenty

48. In general, female arrests   48.____

    A. increase much more slowly than male arrests
    B. are increasing much more quickly than male arrests
    C. are decreasing with respect to male arrests

D. continue to be underrepresented
E. do not lead to incarceration

49. Currently, whites account for *approximately* _____ percent of crime. 49._____
   A. 25   B. 40   C. 50   D. 70   E. 85

50. One factor to be kept in mind in comparing white crime statistics with black crime statistics is that 50._____
   A. blacks comprise 12% of the population
   B. blacks live in urban poverty areas
   C. whites are punished more severely
   D. blacks are punished more severely
   E. whites are racist

KEY (CORRECT ANSWERS)

1. D	11. E	21. C	31. B	41. B
2. D	12. B	22. B	32. C	42. D
3. C	13. B	23. D	33. C	43. C
4. D	14. A	24. E	34. D	44. D
5. C	15. C	25. D	35. C	45. A
6. C	16. D	26. D	36. D	46. E
7. D	17. A	27. E	37. E	47. C
8. C	18. D	28. B	38. D	48. B
9. A	19. C	29. E	39. D	49. D
10. C	20. B	30. E	40. C	50. A

EXAMINATION SECTION
TEST 1

DIRECTIONS: Each question or incomplete statement is followed by several suggested answers or completions. Select the one that BEST answers the question or completes the statement. *PRINT THE LETTER OF THE CORRECT ANSWER IN THE SPACE AT THE RIGHT.*

1. The UNIFORM CRIME REPORTS

   A. take serious note of criminals' social class
   B. take no note of criminals' social class
   C. occasionally record class backgrounds
   D. purposely avoid recording class backgrounds
   E. assume a classless society

2. The concept of "categoric risks," attributed to sociologist Walter Reckless, refers to the
   I. greater likelihood of lower class people to be arrested
   II. greater likelihood of upper class people to be arrested
   III. lack of legal protections in some classes of society
   IV. tendency of judges to be lenient with white people
   V. tendency of rich people to bribe judges

   The CORRECT answer is:

   A. I *only*
   B. I, III
   C. II *only*
   D. II, IV, V
   E. none of the above

3. The President's Commission on Law Enforcement and Administration of Justice found that, as of 1979, UNIFORM CRIME REPORTS

   A. accurately estimate crime
   B. underestimate crime by half
   C. underestimate crime several times
   D. overestimate crimes
   E. are statistically biased

4. A MAJOR source of criminology data comes from the

   A. LEAA   B. NORC   C. UCR   D. FBI   E. CIA

5. The PRIMARY founders of the classical school of criminology were
   I. Oliver Wendell Holmes
   II. Cesar Beccaria
   III. Jeremy Bentham
   IV. Cesare Lombroso
   V. C. Wright Mills

   The CORRECT answer is:

   A. I, II, IV
   B. I, V
   C. II, III
   D. II, IV
   E. III, IV, V

6. Criminologists who explain criminal behavior WITHOUT referring to biological models *usually* refer to
    I. interpersonal relations
    II. socialization
    III. chromosomal variations
    IV. police records
    V. personal experience
   The CORRECT answer is:

   A. I *only*
   B. I, II
   C. III *only*
   D. II, III
   E. IV, V

7. Research shows that
    I. crime and psychological disorders are associated
    II. crime and psychological disorders are not associated
    III. relatively few prisoners are psychotic
    IV. 5% or less of convicted prisoners are psychotic
    V. sane people rarely commit crimes
   The CORRECT answer is:

   A. I *only*
   B. I, V
   C. II, III
   D. II, III, IV
   E. IV, V

8. Psychologists and sociologists researching crime disagree *primarily* on

   A. whether there are criminal personality types
   B. whether statistics can accurately represent real crime
   C. methodological flaws in data collection
   D. interpretation of data
   E. how criminology ought to be taught in college

9. Howard Becker was responsible for popularizing the criminological theory of

   A. labeling
   B. differential association
   C. theory of anomie
   D. subcultural theories
   E. positive reinforcement

10. One can characterize labeling theory informally by saying that
    I. people become criminals by imitating people around them
    II. people tend to fulfill others' expectations of them
    III. social scientists should not label people
    IV. scientific classification helps explain behavior
    V. crime becomes a "self-fulfilling prophecy"
    The CORRECT answer is:

    A. I *only*
    B. II, V
    C. III, IV
    D. IV
    E. V *only*

11. A *primary* concept connected with labeling theory is 11.____

    A. deviance
    B. punishment
    C. classification
    D. ostracism
    E. stereotypes

12. Professor Edwin Sutherland developed the criminological theory of 12.____

    A. labeling
    B. differential association
    C. theory of anomie
    D. subcultural theories
    E. positive reinforcement

13. Emile Durkheim developed the criminological theory of 13.____

    A. labeling
    B. differential association
    C. theory of anomie
    D. subcultural theories
    E. positive reinforcement

14. The Code of Hammurabi is 14.____
    I. a relatively recent sociological phenomenon
    II. traceable to ancient times
    III. identifiable with lex taliones
    IV. an enlightened code
    V. currently popular

    The CORRECT answer is:

    A. I *only*
    B. I, IV
    C. II *only*
    D. II, III
    E. III, V

15. A *primary* concept in the Hammurabi code is 15.____
    I. turning the other cheek to attackers
    II. wreaking revenge on criminals
    III. an eye for an eye
    IV. punishing criminals the way they harmed victims
    V. reform

    The CORRECT answer is:

    A. I *only*
    B. I, V
    C. II, III
    D. II, III, IV
    E. III, IV, V

16. Albert Cohen, besides being noted for his research on juvenile delinquency, is largely responsible for the criminological theory of 16.____

    A. labeling
    B. differential association
    C. theory of anomie
    D. subcultural theories
    E. positive reinforcement

17. The criminal phenomenon *most aptly* explained by differential association theory is 17.____

    A. assault and battery
    B. white collar crime
    C. theft
    D. murder
    E. psychopathic homicide

18. Differential association occurs *primarily* through

    A. media images
    B. affective deviations
    C. intimate groups
    D. role models
    E. economic privation

19. White collar crime includes
    I. false advertising
    II. kickbacks for political favors
    III. fee splitting
    IV. padding expense accounts
    V. lying to the IRS
    The CORRECT answer is:

    A. I, III, IV
    B. II, III
    C. II, III, IV, V
    D. III, IV
    E. all of the above

20. Prosecuting white collar crimes is difficult because
    I. offenders are not often apprehended
    II. offenders have high social status
    III. administrative courts are used rather than criminal courts
    IV. corporations bribe judges
    V. no harm results from white collar crime
    The CORRECT answer is:

    A. I *only*
    B. I, II, V
    C. II, III
    D. II, III, IV
    E. all of the above

21. Contemporary versions of differential association theory emphasize the psychological theories of
    I. Freudian psychoanalysis
    II. behaviorism
    III. operant conditioning
    IV. group therapy
    V. Gestalt psychology
    The CORRECT answer is:

    A. I *only*
    B. II *only*
    C. II, III
    D. IV, V
    E. all of the above

22. One fact that refutes differential association explanations of criminal behavior is that
    I. some individuals use legitimate business skills to commit crimes
    II. some who are conditioned still do not commit crimes
    III. they are formulated too abstractly
    IV. they are difficult to test mathematically
    V. they cannot predict criminal behavior
    The CORRECT answer is:

    A. I *only*
    B. I, II, V
    C. II, III, IV
    D. IV *only*
    E. all of the above

23. The concept of *anomie* means

    A. isolation
    B. loneliness
    C. anonymity
    D. normlessness
    E. deviant

24. Durkheim used the concept of anomie *primarily* to explain

    A. white collar crime
    B. violent crimes
    C. suicide
    D. murder
    E. mass murders

25. Anomie is the result of
    I. divorced families
    II. the lack of integration between goals
    III. the lack of legitimate means to attain goals
    IV. the presence of examples of illegitimate goal-achievement
    V. child abuse

    The CORRECT answer is:

    A. I *only*
    B. I, II
    C. II, III
    D. III *only*
    E. IV, V

26. A good synonym for the criminological term *anomie* is

    A. isolation
    B. discouragement
    C. alienation
    D. ostracism
    E. psychopathology

27. Groups exhibiting behavior associated with anomie are
    I. revolutionary groups
    II. paranoid schizophrenics
    III. suicidal people
    IV. slum dwellers
    V. neurotics

    The CORRECT answer is:

    A. I, III
    B. II, III
    C. II, III, IV
    D. III, V
    E. IV *only*

28. The innovative person who is anomie is one who

    A. rejects the goals, but not the means, of social success
    B. rejects the means, but not the goals, of social success
    C. creates the scheme of a new social order
    D. creates his own, better world
    E. rejects materialism for asceticism

29. Anomie is a useful concept for explaining contemporary crimes of

    A. violence
    B. a white-collar nature
    C. property
    D. aggravated assault
    E. passion

30. Subcultural theories of crime causation stress that
    I. subcultures have deviant norms
    II. subcultures are economically depressed
    III. individual behavior reflects group dynamics
    IV. most crime is committed in subcultures
    V. crimes can be avoided by avoiding subcultures
    The CORRECT answer is:

    A. I only
    B. I, III
    C. II, V
    D. III only
    E. IV, V

31. Members of gangs in the working class do NOT exhibit the middle class characteristics and goals of
    I. suppression of aggression
    II. acquisitiveness
    III. self-reliance
    IV. ambition
    V. projection
    The CORRECT answer is:

    A. I only
    B. I, II, V
    C. II only
    D. II, III
    E. II, III, IV

32. Critics of subcultural theories claim that delinquent gang members
    I. are ambivalent toward middle class goals
    II. act out sublimal fantasies
    III. are victims of social environments
    IV. neutralize and rationalize their actions
    V. become civic leaders later in life
    The CORRECT answer is:

    A. I only
    B. I, II
    C. I, IV
    D. III, IV
    E. II, V

33. Types of subcultures of interest to criminologists include _____ subcultures.
    I. criminal
    II. anomic
    III. conflict
    IV. retreatist
    V. Utopian
    The CORRECT answer is:

    A. I, II
    B. I, III
    C. I, III, IV
    D. II, III, V
    E. III, IV, V

34. Criminal subcultures DIFFER from conflict subcultures in that the former
    I. channel aggression and the latter do not
    II. have role models and the latter do not
    III. are likely to be arrested and the latter are not
    IV. are less likely to engage in gang fights
    V. produce more professional criminals
    The CORRECT answer is:

    A. I only
    B. I, III
    C. II only
    D. II, IV, V
    E. IV, V

35. Penal reform theories rely upon the fundamental claim that
    I. offenders ought to be punished
    II. criminals deserve to be paid back for harm they inflict
    III. penal institutions ought to protect society
    IV. punishment ought to deter crime
    V. prisons ought not to produce worse criminals
    The CORRECT answer is:

    A. I only
    B. I, III
    C. II only
    D. II, III, IV
    E. III, IV, V

36. American Quakers contributed to prison reform by
    I. advocating reforming offenders
    II. discouraging imprisonment
    III. encouraging imprisonment
    IV. supporting rehabilitation
    V. advocating religious conversion
    The CORRECT answer is:

    A. I only
    B. I, III
    C. I, III, IV
    D. II, IV, V
    E. III, V

37. A fundamental concept of American penology, as a result of the Quaker influence, is

    A. revenge
    B. retribution
    C. shame
    D. penitence
    E. pacifism

38. The origin of the word "penitentiary" for prison can be explained by referring to
    I. the idea that offenders should be penitent
    II. the encouragement for prisoners to learn a trade
    III. ancient legal customs of punishment
    IV. lex taliones
    V. English common law
    The CORRECT answer is:

    A. I only
    B. I, II, V
    C. II only
    D. III only
    E. III, IV, V

39. A MAJOR drawback of the Quaker approach to penology was that of

   A. problems prisoners had in groups while incarcerated
   B. offenders who learned new criminal techniques in prison
   C. too much solitary confinement of prisoners
   D. too much reliance on private charity for expenses
   E. offenders refusing to become religious converts

40. A popular administrative plan for penal institutions still in use is called the
   I. silent system
   II. Auburn plan
   III. solitary system
   IV. interactionist plan
   V. cost efficient plan

   The CORRECT answer is:

   A. I only   B. I, II
   C. II only   D. II, IV
   E. III, V

41. Factor(s) that *largely* refute(s) the deterrent effects of capital punishment is(are)
   I. the similarity of murder rates in states both lacking and maintaining capital punishment
   II. the difference in homicide rates between states with and without capital punishment
   III. that no one knows how to completely stop homicide
   IV. that mostly lovers and relatives murder each other
   V. that there will always be murderers

   The CORRECT answer is:

   A. I, V   B. II only
   C. III, IV   D. III, V
   E. IV only

42. Probation consists *primarily* of
   I. the suspension of a sentence
   II. the elimination of a sentence
   III. leniency given because of good behavior
   IV. rewarding compliant prisoners
   V. reducing sentences

   The CORRECT answer is:

   A. I only   B. I, III
   C. II only   D. II, III, V
   E. IV only

43. The origins of American probation in penology are

   A. traceable to rehabilitation theory
   B. largely the result of Bentham's theory
   C. in the tradition of English common law
   D. based on American Puritanism
   E. contrary to English common law

44. Parole DIFFERS from probation in that the
    I. former involves incarcerated prisoners
    II. latter involves incarcerated prisoners
    III. former results from criminal, not administrative, courts
    IV. latter results from criminal, not administrative, courts
    V. former is more humane than the latter
    The CORRECT answer is:

    A. I only
    B. I, IV
    C. II only
    D. III, V
    E. IV, V

45. Currently, prisoners who are released from penal institutions are

    A. released automatically
    B. released long after they are due
    C. released on parole
    D. put on probation
    E. reformed

46. *Disengagement* is a term used by criminologists to refer to processes
    I. resulting in isolation
    II. designed to reduce the number of relationships
    III. resulting in immersion in a social role
    IV. resulting in separation from social roles
    V. in which criminals rationalize their actions
    The CORRECT answer is:

    A. I only
    B. I, II, V
    C. II only
    D. II, III, V
    E. II, IV

47. Continuity theory is an important factor in explaining
    I. adolescent behavior
    II. behavior studied by gerontologists
    III. why people perpetuate habits
    IV. why people become innovative
    V. aberrant behavior
    The CORRECT answer is:

    A. I only
    B. I, III, V
    C. II only
    D. II, III
    E. IV only

48. Offenders convicted of crimes ought to be
    I. incarcerated in local jails
    II. incarcerated in prisons
    III. protected from mass murderers
    IV. granted medical care
    V. shot at dawn
    The CORRECT answer is:

    A. I only
    B. II only
    C. II, III
    D. II, IV
    E. V only

49. One of the *fundamental* concepts of American criminal procedures is
    I. due process
    II. administrative efficiency
    III. rex taliones
    IV. presumption of innocence
    V. experts' opinions

    The CORRECT answer is:

    A. I *only*
    B. I, II
    C. I, IV
    D. III
    E. IV, V

50. A concept originating in Roman law and affecting American criminal legislation based on English common law is

    A. nonage
    B. tort
    C. death penalty
    D. discretion
    E. probation

KEY (CORRECT ANSWERS)

1. B	11. A	21. C	31. E	41. A
2. B	12. B	22. E	32. C	42. B
3. C	13. C	23. D	33. C	43. C
4. A	14. D	24. C	34. D	44. B
5. C	15. D	25. C	35. E	45. C
6. B	16. D	26. C	36. C	46. E
7. D	17. B	27. A	37. D	47. D
8. A	18. C	28. B	38. A	48. D
9. A	19. E	29. C	39. C	49. C
10. B	20. C	30. B	40. B	50. A

EXAMINATION SECTION
TEST 1

DIRECTIONS: Each question or incomplete statement is followed by several suggested answers or completions. Select the one that BEST answers the question or completes the statement. *PRINT THE LETTER OF THE CORRECT ANSWER IN THE SPACE AT THE RIGHT.*

1. Under federal laws, a victim is entitled to certain information during the prosecution and trial phase of the proceedings. Notice of _____ is NOT specified by federal law as information to which a victim is entitled.

    A. a plea of guilty or *nolo contendere* by the offender
    B. the sentence imposed on the offender
    C. the arrest of a suspected offender
    D. the status of an investigation, including all unpursued leads

2. In victims' rights law, *compensation* refers to

    A. the requirement that an offender must repay the victim
    B. the settlement of a civil claim filed through the courts
    C. money paid to a crime victim through state victim assistance programs
    D. the payment of a civil claim by a third party found to be jointly responsible for an offense

3. It is generally believed that the primary reason for the victims' rights movement in the United States has been

    A. the increasing extent of cultural problems, such as drug abuse, which leave victims at the mercy of deviant behavior
    B. the traditional practice of the criminal justice system to consider all crimes to be crimes against society, and therefore excluding victims from participating in criminal proceedings
    C. the rise of a celebrity culture which tends to transform the most violent criminals into important public figures
    D. an overall increase in crime statistics

4. Which of the following psychological theories BEST explains why participating in the criminal justice system is stressful for victims of crime?

    A. Classical conditioning theory
    B. Humanism
    C. Behaviorism
    D. Cognitive theory

5. For purposes of characterization, stalkers are generally divided into two groups: love obsession stalkers and simple obsession stalkers. Most likely to describe a love obsession stalker is one who

    A. has recently been rejected by a long-standing partner
    B. has been involved in a brief but unsuccessful relationship with the victim
    C. feels the need to control the victim through intimidation and/or violence
    D. is fixated on an individual with whom he has no relationship

6. Which of the following statements is TRUE?

    A. Adolescents have slightly lower rates of assault than young adults or other Americans.
    B. 12-19 year olds are at least twice as likely as those over 20 to become victims of personal crime.
    C. About 60% of all forcible rape cases occurred when the victim was under 18 years of age.
    D. The lifetime risk of homicide is slightly higher for men than for women.

7. Which of the following is a role and responsibility of law enforcement officials to victims of crime?

    A. Providing notification of case status at key stages of the criminal justice system
    B. Providing referrals and accompaniment to crisis intervention and psychological first aid
    C. Courtroom orientation
    D. Helping the victim to compose a victim impact statement

8. The right to _____ is typically NOT a right that is provided for in most victims' rights legislation.

    A. be notified of court proceedings
    B. restitution
    C. compel prosecution of an offender regardless of the wishes of prosecutors
    D. be present at all public court proceedings related to the offense

9. Approximately what percentage of all rape victims are reported to develop what is known as rape-related post-traumatic stress disorder (RR-PTSD)?

    A. 10   B. 33   C. 50   D. 90

10. The content of victims' rights legislation at both the federal and state level can be understood in four general categories. Which of the following is NOT one of these?

    A. Providing specific victims' rights
    B. Providing more direct victim participation in investigating and prosecuting crimes
    C. Requiring victim services or assistance
    D. Reform measures making the criminal justice system more victim-oriented

11. The PRIMARY goal of crisis intervention can best be described as

    A. protecting the victim from a situation in which he or she has become more likely to experience a traumatic event than other people
    B. helping the victim to identify and endure the long-term consequences of a traumatic event
    C. protecting a victim from self-harm following a traumatic event
    D. helping the victim to identify and cope with the sense of *disequilibrium* in the aftermath of a trauma

12. Each of the following are common physical symptoms of post-traumatic stress disorder (PTSD) EXCEPT

    A. inability to sleep/fitful sleep   B. difficulty concentrating
    C. severe headaches   D. irritability

13. Which of the following crimes generally has the highest annual victim costs, at a 1996 figure of $127 billion per year?

    A. Child abuse
    B. Rape
    C. Assault
    D. Murder

14. The preponderance of hate crimes committed in the United States are directed against

    A. male homosexuals
    B. blacks
    C. whites
    D. Jews

15. According to Robert's seven-stage crisis intervention model, which of the following procedures in a crisis intervention is typically performed FIRST?

    A. Establishing rapport with the victim
    B. Identifying major problems
    C. Planning and conducting a thorough assessment
    D. Dealing with feelings and emotions

16. Each of the following is considered to be a role and responsibility of prosecutors to victims of crime EXCEPT

    A. providing intervention and protection to victims and witnesses who are being intimidated or harassed
    B. offering employer, landlord, or creditor intervention services
    C. offering assistance to victims in completing victim compensation applications
    D. incorporating any victim impact statement into the pre-sentence investigation (PSI) to the court

17. Which of the following is most likely to be a behavioral indicator of child neglect?

    A. Head banging
    B. Lethargy
    C. Eating disorders
    D. Hyperactivity

18. The purpose of *Megan's Law* is to

    A. allow victims to seek civil damages from offenders, whether the offenders have been convicted or not
    B. allow victims to be present in every stage of a criminal court proceeding
    C. protect communities from potential harm by convicted sex offenders
    D. prevent criminals from gaining financial profit from their offenses

19. In order for a crime victim to be paid by a state victim assistance program, most states require each of the following EXCEPT the

    A. victim must not have expenses covered by another source, i.e., an insurance company
    B. victim must provide proof of losses
    C. offender must at least be arrested for the crime
    D. victim must have reported the crime to law enforcement officials within 48 hours of its occurrence

20. In general, applications for monetary payments from state victim assistance programs must be made

   A. in the state where the offense occurred
   B. in the state where the victim resides
   C. in person before an organized board
   D. within 3 months of an offense

21. Which of the following expenses is LEAST likely to be covered by state victim assistance programs?

   A. Funeral expenses
   B. Psychological treatment and counseling
   C. Punitive damages for pain and suffering
   D. Lost wages

22. Which of the following is/are mandates of the Victims of Child Abuse Act of 1990?
   I. Permitting testimony via two-way closed circuit television in certain circumstances
   II. Limiting the scope of competency examinations for children unless ordered by a judge
   III. Consultation with multi-disciplinary teams for information on professional evaluations
   IV. Accompaniment throughout the trial by an adult attendant
   The CORRECT answer is:

   A. I, III
   B. I, IV
   C. II, III, IV
   D. I, II, III, IV

23. Generally, post-traumatic stress disorder (PTSD) is defined as acute if it lasts for fewer than _____ following the traumatic event.

   A. 1 month
   B. 3 months
   C. 6 months
   D. 1 year

24. When the first state victims' rights laws were first developed in the 1980s, victims of _____ were the most likely to have been excluded from protection.

   A. child abuse
   B. domestic abuse
   C. drunk driving
   D. assault

25. Each of the following is a guideline for a victim assistant's participation in crisis intervention procedures EXCEPT

   A. expressing empathy by saying things such as *I understand*
   B. asking the victim to describe the event
   C. letting the victim talk for as long as he or she likes without interruption
   D. asking the victim to describe his or her reactions and responses

KEY (CORRECT ANSWERS)

1.	D	11.	D
2.	C	12.	C
3.	B	13.	B
4.	A	14.	B
5.	D	15.	C
6.	B	16.	D
7.	B	17.	B
8.	C	18.	C
9.	B	19.	C
10.	B	20.	A

21. C
22. D
23. B
24. C
25. A

TEST 2

DIRECTIONS: Each question or incomplete statement is followed by several suggested answers or completions. Select the one that BEST answers the question or completes the statement. *PRINT THE LETTER OF THE CORRECT ANSWER IN THE SPACE AT THE RIGHT.*

1. Which of the following is/are generally considered to be goals of advocacy for victims of domestic violence?
    I. Increase victims' ability to make a successful transition to independence
    II. Empower women to make significant changes and solve problems
    III. Connect the victim with community resources, both short- and long-term
    IV. Insure the prosecution and punishment of the batterer
   The CORRECT answer is:

   A. II, III
   B. I, II, III
   C. II, III, IV
   D. I, III, IV

2. It is generally LEAST appropriate for a victim to read an impact statement _____ hearing.

   A. at an arraignment
   B. during a sentencing
   C. during a restorative justice
   D. during a parole

3. Which of the following is a role and responsibility of judges to victims of crime?

   A. Expediting the prompt return of property
   B. Providing information and referrals to victims who require assistance
   C. Ordering restitution payments that receive priority above fines and other offender obligations
   D. Providing notification of case status at key stages in the criminal justice process

4. Which of the following is an important difference between restitution and compensation? The payment of

   A. compensation is usually associated with criminal, rather than civil, proceedings
   B. restitution requires that the offender be convicted
   C. restitution requires proof of losses
   D. compensation may involve punitive damages

5. Statistics generally show that in abusive domestic relationships, a woman's risk of homicide is greatest

   A. when she is living with the man
   B. when children are not present
   C. in the first two months of any separation
   D. immediately following an instance of acute battering

6. Which of the following is LEAST likely to be a crime whose victim would be eligible for payment by a state victim assistance program?

   A. Assault and battery
   B. Domestic abuse
   C. Robbery
   D. Child abuse

7. Which of the following is most likely to be a physical indicator of child emotional abuse?

   A. Unexplained bruises
   B. Inappropriate clothing for weather conditions
   C. Below-average height and weight
   D. Speech disorders

8. Which of the following is/are factors which place a man at risk as a potential batterer?
   I. Drug or alcohol use
   II. 30-45 years of age
   III. Witnessing spousal abuse among parents
   IV. Poverty

   The CORRECT answer is:

   A. I, III
   B. I, II, IV
   C. I, III, IV
   D. II, III, IV

9. Which of the following types of mental health professionals is LEAST likely to have received graduate-level training?

   A. Clinical mental health counselor
   B. Marriage and family therapist
   C. Clinical social worker
   D. Clinical psychologist

10. Which of the following is generally not a party that is considered to be involved in the phenomenon known as *secondary victimization*?

    A. Victim's family and friends
    B. The criminal justice system
    C. The offender
    D. Victim compensation programs

11. In a case in which a victim seeks to have the court force public officials to provide them with adequate and reasonable compliance with their legislated rights, which of the following legal instruments is appropriate?

    A. Writ of mandamus
    B. Order of injunction
    C. Writ of a certiorari
    D. Writ of execution

12. In most situations, a victim's first contact with the criminal justice system is through

    A. the victim's own attorney
    B. the court
    C. law enforcement
    D. the prosecutor

13. Studies of women who are involved in abusive relationships show that they are generally NOT likely to

    A. believe she can change the batterer's behavior
    B. exhibit consistent patterns of behavior
    C. feel shame or guilt
    D. express a fear of staying with the batterer

14. Which of the following is a role and responsibility of probation officials to victims of crime?

    A. Soliciting victim's opinions relevant to appropriate community service sanctions for the offender
    B. Contacting victim service professionals to provide on-site support
    C. Providing orientation to the criminal justice process
    D. Providing educational and accompaniment programs to familiarize victims with the courtroom

15. Which of the following is a guideline for domestic violence victim validation?

    A. Downplay the widespread prevalence of such crimes among all women
    B. Avoid speaking directly about the violence
    C. Stress the criminal nature of the violence and the fact that the victim is not to blame
    D. Seek verification of the victim's story from second parties

16. A counselor is unable to convince a victim of domestic violence to leave her situation. Which of the following are strategies the victim should be advised to use in this case?
    I. Fight back when the behavior begins, to make violence more difficult
    II. Stay away from children during an abusive episode
    III. Purchase a defensive device such as mace or a *stun gun* in case the violence escalates to a level that is life-threatening
    IV. Conceal the abuse as much as possible from family and friends
    The CORRECT answer is:

    A. I, III   B. II only   C. II, IV   D. III, IV

17. The purpose of statutes known as *Son of Sam* laws is to

    A. allow victims to seek civil damages from offenders, whether the offenders have been convicted or not
    B. allow victims to be present in every stage of a criminal court proceeding
    C. protect communities from potential harm by convicted sex offenders
    D. prevent criminals from gaining financial profit from their offenses

18. Which of the following is NOT considered to be a general factor involved in the function of crisis intervention?

    A. Establishing a long-term therapeutic relationship
    B. Focusing on coping strategies and problem-solving behavior
    C. Resolving immediate problems associated with crime victimization
    D. A high level of therapist activity marshaling all resources to facilitate client readjustment

19. Which of the following is a demographic trend in the occurrence of child abuse?

    A. Boys are more likely to suffer death or serious injury as a result of abuse.
    B. Sexual abuse generally begins at the onset of puberty.
    C. Boys are more likely to be abused by males outside the family.
    D. Girls are only slightly more likely to be sexually abused than boys.

20. Which of the following is not generally considered to be a role or responsibility of institutional corrections to victims of crime?

    A. Upon request, notifying victims of an offender's status
    B. Implementing and monitoring victim/offender programs such as victim impact panels
    C. Contacting victims to assess the psychological, financial, and physical impact of the crime
    D. Obtaining relevant victim information from court documentation for inclusion in the offender's file

21. In victims' rights law, *restitution* refers to

    A. the requirement that an offender must repay the victim
    B. the settlement of a civil claim filed through the courts
    C. money paid to a crime victim through state victim assistance programs
    D. the payment of a civil claim by a third party found to be jointly responsible for an offense

22. Which of the following is/are principles that should guide an advocate's attempts to communicate with a child victim?
    I. Avoid the *old* and *young* classification
    II. Children seem indifferent to whether they've impressed adults or not
    III. Young children tend to repeat the end of a prior sentence if they are unsure of an answer
    IV. The use of pronouns is often confusing to children

    The CORRECT answer is:

    A. I *only*
    B. I, III, IV
    C. II, III
    D. III, IV

23. An offender is described as *judgment proof* if he or she

    A. has committed at least three felony offenses in the last 10 years
    B. has an unassailable alibi to the crime
    C. has committed a capital crime in a state that does not impose capital punishment
    D. does not have any financial resources or assets against which a monetary judgment can be enforced

24. Which of the following is a cognitive symptom of anxiety?

    A. Insomnia
    B. Rapid heart rate
    C. Impaired social functioning
    D. Feelings of terror or helplessness

25. Which of the following types of victims are LEAST likely to be protected by confidentiality statutes?

    A. Child victims
    B. Relatives of murder victims
    C. Victims of domestic violence
    D. Victims of rape and sexual assault

KEY (CORRECT ANSWERS)

1. B
2. A
3. C
4. B
5. C

6. C
7. D
8. C
9. A
10. C

11. A
12. C
13. B
14. A
15. C

16. B
17. D
18. A
19. A
20. C

21. A
22. B
23. D
24. D
25. B

TEST 3

DIRECTIONS: Each question or incomplete statement is followed by several suggested answers or completions. Select the one that BEST answers the question or completes the statement. *PRINT THE LETTER OF THE CORRECT ANSWER IN THE SPACE AT THE RIGHT.*

1. A model domestic violence response should include
    I. Joint custody arrangements
    II. Mediation between victims and perpetrators
    III. Mutual restraining orders
    IV. Couples therapy
   The CORRECT answer is:

   A. I, IV
   B. II, III
   C. II only
   D. None of the above

2. Each of the following states includes *Good Samaritans* who intervene in crimes to apply for monetary payment from victim assistance programs EXCEPT

   A. Georgia
   B. Ohio
   C. New York
   D. South Dakota

3. Which of the following types of crime is most likely to have a widespread impact on the victim's community?

   A. Hate or bias crime
   B. Sexual assault
   C. Stalking
   D. Workplace violence

4. In most cases, the first symptom of rape-related post-traumatic stress disorder (RR-PTSD) is

   A. avoidance behavior
   B. feelings of reliving the traumatic experience
   C. memory impairment
   D. social withdrawal

5. Which of the following is a role and responsibility of parole officials to victims of crime?

   A. Implementing and monitoring victim/offender programming such as conciliation
   B. Providing information to crime victims about their statutory rights
   C. Offering assistance to victims in completing victim compensation applications
   D. Continuing restitution orders emanating from a judge

6. Each of the following are common psychological symptoms of post-traumatic stress disorder (PTSD) EXCEPT

   A. antisocial behavior
   B. decreased ability to feel emotions
   C. inability to remember parts of the traumatic event
   D. detachment from persons or activities which were formerly important to the victim

7. Of substantiated cases of child abuse, most victims suffer from

   A. emotional maltreatment
   B. sexual abuse
   C. neglect
   D. physical abuse

8. Guidelines for victims of domestic violence who plan to leave an abusive situation include
   I. contacting a local shelter for information about rights, financial assistance, and counseling
   II. maintaining a journal of all violent incidents
   III. seeking an alternative means of support for the abandoned spouse
   IV. practicing an escape plan in case the need arises

   The CORRECT answer is:

   A. I, IV
   B. I, II, IV
   C. I, III, IV
   D. II, III, IV

9. The primary elements in most stalking statutes include each of the following EXCEPT

   A. the defendant has intent and/or apparent ability to carry out a threat
   B. the behavior is threatening
   C. a requirement that the behavior continues after it has been reported to law enforcement
   D. the crime involves a series of acts over a period of time

10. A crime victim would generally remain eligible for monetary payment from a state victim assistance program in cases where the victim

    A. does not meet a financial-needs test
    B. has previously been convicted of a felony
    C. was involved in committing a crime when he or she was victimized
    D. declines to cooperate with law enforcement officials in the criminal proceedings

11. The PRIMARY reason for the increasing push toward police-level victim services is that

    A. the police are in most cases the most offender-centered arm of the criminal justice system
    B. in a large majority of crimes no perpetrator is apprehended, and the case never goes to court
    C. they generally have more time to deal with the problems of victims than members of the court
    D. police generally require the greatest degree of sensitivity training among members of the criminal justice system

12. A case of post-traumatic stress disorder (PTSD) is described as *delayed onset* if symptoms do not surface until after _____ or more have passed since the traumatic event.

    A. 1 month
    B. 3 months
    C. 6 months
    D. 1 year

13. Which of the following is most likely to be a behavioral indicator of child physical abuse?

    A. Chronic fatigue
    B. Frequent tantrums
    C. Thumbsucking in older children
    D. Suggesting other children be punished harshly

14. According to stress theory, which of the following types of stressors are likely to impact victims of crime in particular?
    I. Chronic
    II. Routine
    III. Developmental
    IV. Catastrophic

    The CORRECT answer is:

    A. I only   B. II, III   C. I, IV   D. IV only

15. A victim seeks to delay sentencing hearings for an offender until he or she has completed a victim impact statement. Which of the following legal instruments is most appropriate for this purpose?

    A. Writ of mandamus
    B. Order of injunction
    C. Writ of a certiorari
    D. Order of estoppel

16. The typical elderly victim of crime is likely to be each of the following EXCEPT

    A. over the age of 75
    B. an apartment dweller
    C. separated or divorced
    D. a racial or ethnic minority

17. Which of the following statements about post-traumatic stress disorder (PTSD) is TRUE?

    A. Rates are higher among white victims than those of other racial categories.
    B. PTSD symptoms lasting longer than a few months are rare.
    C. It is more prevalent among crime victims than among victims of other traumatic events.
    D. Rates among victims who do not report crimes to the criminal justice system are slightly higher than among those who do.

18. If a victim seeks a civil ruling against an offender who has no assets, the first and best option for the victim is to

    A. file a claim for the punitive amount with the state victims' compensation authority
    B. seek a judgment against a third party who may be held jointly responsible
    C. make the offender into a garnishee
    D. rely solely on the criminal justice system

19. According to Roberts' seven-stage crisis intervention model, which of the following procedures in a crisis intervention is typically performed LAST?

    A. Generating and exploring alternatives
    B. Developing and formulating an action plan
    C. Identifying major problems
    D. Planning and conducting a thorough assessment

20. Each of the following is an expense that is likely to be covered by a court-ordered restitution EXCEPT

    A. the cost of property damage
    B. lost wages
    C. out-of-pocket costs such as medical expenses
    D. child support (for rape victims)

21. Which of the following crimes occurs most commonly on United States college campuses?

    A. Aggravated assault
    B. Rape
    C. Burglary
    D. Non-forcible sexual assault

22. Statistics demonstrate that the most likely victim of sexual assault is a female who
    I. works in the evening or late hours
    II. is between the ages of 16 and 19
    III. comes from a low-income household
    IV. lives in an urban area
    The CORRECT answer is:

    A. I, IV
    B. II, III
    C. II, III, IV
    D. II, IV

23. When leaving a violent domestic situation behind, a victim should generally do each of the following EXCEPT

    A. provide relatives with relocation information
    B. avoid the use of credit cards
    C. take all important documents upon departure
    D. ask the police to supervise as belongings are removed, and to escort the departure

24. For most victims, the most common response to crime-related conditioned stimuli is

    A. flashbacks
    B. detachment
    C. amnesia of certain parts of the traumatic event
    D. avoidance behavior

25. The most commonly occurring violent hate crime in the United States is

    A. simple assault
    B. murder
    C. intimidation
    D. forcible rape

KEY (CORRECT ANSWERS)

1.	D	11.	B
2.	C	12.	C
3.	A	13.	D
4.	B	14.	C
5.	D	15.	B
6.	A	16.	A
7.	C	17.	C
8.	B	18.	B
9.	C	19.	B
10.	B	20.	D

21. C
22. C
23. A
24. D
25. C

READING COMPREHENSION
UNDERSTANDING AND INTERPRETING WRITTEN MATERIAL
EXAMINATION SECTION
TEST 1

DIRECTIONS: Each question or incomplete statement is followed by several suggested answers or completions. Select the one that BEST answers the question or completes the statement. *PRINT THE LETTER OF THE CORRECT ANSWER IN THE SPACE AT THE RIGHT.*

Questions 1-6.

DIRECTIONS: Questions 1 through 6 are to be answered SOLELY on the basis of the following passage.

Delinquency and crime and reactions to them are social products and are socially defined. Society, as a whole, not individuals, creates and defines rules, pejoratively labels those who break rules, and prescribes ways for reacting to the labeled person. Moreover, at times the societal process of defining, labeling, and reacting may not affect behavior but at other times it is influential in determining both who shall enter the correctional process and what its outcome will be.

What's more, the labeling process is often a means of isolating offenders from, rather than integrating them in, effective participation in such major societal institutions as schools, businesses, unions, and political, community, and fraternal organizations. These institutions are the major access routes to a successful, non-delinquent career. Those who are in power in them are the gatekeepers of society and, if offenders and correctional programs are isolated from them, then the personal wishes and characteristics of offenders will have little bearing on whether correctional programs succeed or fail.

1. According to the above passage, the MAJOR determinant of whether an offender will succeed in society is his
   A. self-confidence and general intelligence
   B. degree of participation in the major societal institutions
   C. attitude toward the entire criminal justice system
   D. overall criminal record

1.____

2. The above passage suggests that the isolation of offenders from certain groups within society through the labeling process is
   A. intentional   B. unlawful   C. beneficial   D. irreversible

2.____

3. Of the following, the MOST appropriate title for the passage is
   A. Methods of Reforming the Attitudes of Society
   B. Unjust Justice
   C. Delinquency and Crime
   D. Society's Rejection of Offenders

3.____

4. According to the passage, delinquency and crime are created by the
   A. characteristics of offenders
   B. correctional process itself
   C. operations of society
   D. gatekeepers of major institutions

5. Of the following suggested methods of helping offenders adjust to society, the one which the passage would be LEAST likely to favor would be to
   A. establish cooperative relations between correctional programs in cooperation with influential members of society
   B. keep the public informed of current developments in the corrections field by contributing information to local newspapers
   C. create an organizational structure within correctional institutions which, wherever practicable, resembles life in society
   D. encourage offenders to maintain close ties with other offenders with whom they become friendly while incarcerated

6. According to the passage, the rehabilitation of the offender is MOST likely to be determined by
   A. the individual inmate himself
   B. dynamic reformation programs
   C. society as a whole
   D. the specific correctional institution

Questions 7-10.

DIRECTIONS: Questions 7 through 10 are to be answered SOLELY on the basis of the following passage.

Urban crime rates are generally higher than those prevailing in rural areas. This apparent preponderance of urban crime has been observed by many criminologists both here and abroad and, although the factual basis for their conclusion that more crime occurs in urban areas does not lend itself to close measurement, there seems to be sufficient reason to accept it at face value. But there is an increasing body of evidence accumulating in the United States indicative that a profound change in these relationships may be in progress. For murder and rape, the rural crime rate of this country now equals the urban rate. As to all homicides, it exceeds the urban crime rate of the New England, Middle Atlantic, and North Central states, and shows such impressive advances for aggravated assault and robbery as to greatly reduce the former disparity. Such changes raise the question whether rural crimes, reacting to new means of transport and consequent interchange of population, which are urban influences, may not now be in the process of attaining urban crime levels. Certain it is that crimes against the person have for centuries been relatively more numerous in rural areas than crimes against property. Hence, the new trend is in a sense an extension of a condition of long standing.

7. According to the above passage, the statement that crime rates are generally higher in urban areas than in rural areas
   A. has not been definitely established although there is strong evidence to support such a view
   B. is justified but does not necessarily indicate that more crime is actually committed in urban areas

C. has been definitely established despite some contrary evidence submitted by criminologists
D. is not justified since the facts gathered by many criminologists do not lend themselves to close measurement

8. Concerning the present relationship between rural and urban crime rates, it would be MOST correct to state, according to the above passage, that for   8.____
   A. aggravated assault and robbery, the urban rate remained stationary while the rural rate increased
   B. murder and rape, the rural rate equals the urban rate in the Middle Atlantic states
   C. aggravated assault and robbery, the rural rate was formerly lower than the urban rate
   D. murder and rape, the urban rate is less than the rural rate in the North Central states

9. The development of new means of transport, according to the above passage,   9.____
   A. may or may not be an urban influence but it definitely contributed to a rise in rural crime levels
   B. is an urban influence and may or may not contribute to a rise in rural crime levels
   C. may or may not be an urban influence and may or may not contribute to a rise in rural crime levels
   D. is an urban influence and has definitely contributed to a rise in rural crime levels

10. The new trend is BEST defined, according to the above passage, as a tendency for crime against   10.____
    A. the person to be more numerous in rural areas than they have been in the past in urban areas
    B. property to be less numerous in urban areas than they are in rural areas
    C. the person to be more numerous in rural areas than they have been in the past
    D. property to be more numerous in urban areas than they have been in urban areas

Questions 11-15.

DIRECTIONS: Questions 11 through 15 are to be answered SOLELY on the basis of the following passage.

If we are to study crime in its widest social setting, we will find a variety of conduct which, although criminal in the legal sense, is not offensive to the moral conscience of a considerable number of persons. Traffic violations for example, do not brand the offender as guilty of moral offense. In fact, the recipient of a traffic ticket is usually simply the subject of some good-natured joking by his friends. Although there may be indignation among certain groups of citizens against gambling and liquor law violations, these activities are often tolerated, if not openly supported, by the more numerous residents of the community. Indeed, certain social and service clubs regularly conduct gambling games and lotteries for the purpose of raising funds. Some communities regard violations involving the sale of liquor with little concern in order to profit from increased license fees and taxes paid by dealers. The thousand and one forms of political graft and corruption which infest our urban centers only occasionally arouse public condemnation and official action.

11. According to the above passage, all types of illegal conduct are 11._____
    A. condemned by all elements of the community
    B. considered a moral offense, although some are tolerated by a few citizens
    C. violations of the law, but some are acceptable to certain elements of the community
    D. found in a social setting which is not punishable by law

12. According to the above paragraph, traffic violations are GENERALLY considered by society as 12._____
    A. crimes requiring the maximum penalty set by the law
    B. more serious than violations of the liquor laws
    C. offenses against the morals of the community
    D. relatively minor offenses requiring minimum punishment

13. According to the above passage, a lottery conducted for the purpose of raising funds for a church 13._____
    A. is considered a serious violation of law
    B. may be tolerated by a community which has laws against gambling
    C. may be conducted under special laws demanded by the more numerous residents
    D. arouses indignation in most communities

14. On the basis of the passage, the MOST likely reaction in the community to a police raid on a gambling casino would be 14._____
    A. more an attitude of indifference than interest in the raid
    B. general approval of the raid
    C. condemnation of the raid by most people
    D. demand for further action, since this raid is not sufficient to end gambling activities

15. The one of the following which BEST describes the central thought of this passage and would be MOST suitable as a title for it is 15._____
    A. Crime and the Police
    B. Public condemnation of Graft and Corruption
    C. Gambling is Not Always a Vicious Business
    D. Public Attitude Toward Law Violations

Questions 16-18.

DIRECTIONS: Questions 16 through 18 are to be answered SOLELY on the basis of the following passage.

The rise of urban-industrial society has complicated the social arrangements needed to regulate contacts between people. As a consequence, there has been an unprecedented increase in the volume of laws and regulations designed to control individual conduct and to govern the relationship of the individual to others. In a century there has been an eight-fold increase in the crimes for which one may be prosecuted.

For these offenses, the courts have the ultimate responsibility for redressing wrongs and convicting the guilty. The body of legal precepts gives the impression of an abstract and even-handed dispensation of justice. Actually, the personnel of the agencies applying these precept are faced with the difficulties of fitting abstract principles to highly variable situations emerging from the dynamics of everyday life. It is inevitable that discrepancies should exist between precept and practice.

The legal institutions serve as a framework for the social order by their slowness to respond to the caprices of transitory fad. This valuable contribution exacts a price in terms of the inflexibility of legal institutions in responding to new circumstances. This possibility is promoted by the changes in values and norms of the dynamic larger culture of which the legal precepts are a part.

16. According to the above passage, the increase in the number of laws and regulations during the twentieth century can be attributed to the
    A. complexity of modern industrial society
    B. increased seriousness of offenses committed
    C. growth of individualism
    D. anonymity of urban living

17. According to the above passage, which of the following presents a problem to the staff of legal agencies?
    A. The need to eliminate the discrepancy between precept and practice
    B. The necessity to apply abstract legal precepts to rapidly changing conditions
    C. The responsibility for reducing the number of abstract legal principles
    D. The responsibility for understanding offenses in terms of the real life situations from which they emerge

18. According to the above passage, it can be concluded that legal institutions affect social institutions by
    A. preventing change
    B. keeping pace with its norms and values
    C changing its norms and values
    D. providing stability

Questions 19-21.

DIRECTIONS: Questions 19 through 21 are to be answered SOLELY on the basis of the following passage.

This research lends additional emphasis to the contention that crime, as reported and recorded in the United States, is largely a function of social and cultural factors rather than biological, psychological, or entirely chance of factors. In the absence of significant biological variations or significant differences in basic mental processes on a regional or sectional basis, all other things being equal, one would expect a rather even crime rate from state to state. Since vast differences in crime rates on a sectional basis are found to persist over a period of time, one may hypothesize that subcultural variations of a regional or sectional nature are responsible for these regional or sectional patterns of crime. Even if this hypothesis cannot be accepted due to underreporting of crime, the least that the data may be said to demonstrate is a distinctly sectional variation in reporting and recording practices, indicating great disparities in sectional reactions to various types of human, or more specifically, criminal behavior.

19. According to the above passage, sectional crime rates
    A. are not affected significantly by entirely chance factors in the absence of psychological factors
    B. can be affected by biological variations or differences in basic mental processes
    C. vary little with significant biological factors in the population
    D. vary significantly in the absence of variable social and cultural factors

20. According to the above passage, great differences in the crime pattern and incidence in different sections of the United States may be said to be, assuming adequate reporting,
    A. a function of sectional variations in reporting and recording practices
    B. based on the specificity of some types of criminal behavior and the lack of a pattern in others
    C. based primarily on differences in the extent of urbanization of the population
    D. the result of regional cultural variations that are persistent over a period of time

21. According to the above passage, the statement that is MOST acceptable concerning the interpretation of crime data distribution by states or regions is that
    A. a more or less even crime rate from state to state indicates absence of significant biological variations
    B. consistent patterns of crime incidence are solely attributable to similar cultural and social factors
    C. failure to report crime that has occurred is indicative of differences in reaction to different types of crimes committed
    D. uniform reporting practices tend to eliminate sectional disparities in causality of crime

Questions 22-26.

DIRECTIONS: Questions 22 through 26 are to be answered SOLELY on the basis of the following passage.

Criminals were once considered sinners who chose to offend against the laws of God and man. They were severely punished for their crimes. Modern criminologists regard society itself as in large part responsible for the crimes committed against it. Poverty, poor living conditions, and inadequate education are all causes of crime. Crime is fundamentally the result of society's failure to provide a decent life for all the people. It is especially common in times when values are changing, as after a war, or in countries where people of different backgrounds and values are thrown together, as in the United States. Crimes, generally speaking, are fewer in countries where there is a settled way of life and a traditional respect for law.

22. This passage deals with
    A. criminals
    B. society
    C. the reasons for crime
    D. crime in the United States

22._____

23. The MAIN idea of this passage is that
    A. crime is common when values are changing
    B. crime is the result of poverty
    C. traditional respect for law prevents a crime
    D. society is largely responsible for crime

23._____

24. According to the passage, which is NOT a cause of crime?
    A. Poverty
    B. Wickedness
    C. Ethnic mixing
    D. Unsettled way of life

24._____

25. Crime is MOST common in
    A. periods of instability
    B. the United States
    C. wartime
    D. suburbs

25._____

26. To prevent crime, the author implies that society should
    A. provide stiffer penalties for criminals
    B. provide a decent way of life are everyone
    C. segregate the poor
    D. give broader powers to the police

26._____

Questions 27-30.

DIRECTIONS: Questions 27 through 30 are to be answered SOLELY on the basis of the following passage.

Perpetrators of crimes are often described by witnesses or victims in terms of salient facial features. The Bertillon System of identification which preceded the widespread use of fingerprints was based on body measurements. Recently, there have been developments in the quantification of procedures used in the classification and comparison of facial characteristics. Devices are now available which enable a trained operator, with the aid of a witness, to form a composite picture of a suspect's face and to translate that composite into a numerical code. Further developments in this area are possible, using computers to develop efficient sequences of questions so that witnesses may quickly arrive at the proper description.

Recent studies of voice analysis and synthesis, originally motivated by problems of efficient telephone transmission, have led to the development of the audio-frequency profile or *voice print*. Each voice print may be sufficiently unique to permit development of a classification system that will make possible identification of the source of a voice print. This method of identification, using an expert to identify the voice patterns, has been introduced in more than 40 cases by 15 different police departments. As with all identification systems that rely on experts to perform the identification, controlled laboratory tests are needed to establish with care the relative frequency of errors of omission and commission made by experts.

27. The MOST appropriate title for the above passage is
    A. Technology in Modern Investigative Detection
    B. Identification By Physical Features
    C. Verification of Identifications By Experts
    D. The Use of Electronic Identification Techniques

    27._____

28. According to the above passage, computers may be used in conjunction with which of the following identification techniques?
    A. Fingerprints
    B. Bertillon System
    C. Voice prints
    D. Composite Facial Pictures

    28._____

29. According to the above passage, the ability to identify individuals based on facial characteristics has improved as a result of
    A. an increase in the number of facial types which can be shown to witnesses
    B. information which is derived from other body measurements
    C. coded classification and comparison techniques
    D. greater reliance upon experts to make the identifications

    29._____

30. According to the above passage, it is CORRECT to state that audio-frequency profiles or voice prints
    A. have been decisive in many prosecutions
    B. reduce the number of errors made by experts
    C. developed as a result of problems in telephonic communications
    D. are unlikely to result in positive identifications

    30._____

KEY (CORRECT ANSWERS)

1.	B	11.	C	21.	C
2.	A	12.	D	22.	C
3.	D	13.	B	23.	A
4.	C	14.	A	24.	B
5.	D	15.	D	25.	A
6.	C	16.	A	26.	B
7.	B	17.	B	27.	B
8.	C	18.	D	28.	D
9.	D	19.	D	29.	C
10.	C	20.	D	30.	C

TEST 2

DIRECTIONS: Each question or incomplete statement is followed by several suggested answers or completions. Select the one that BEST answers the question or completes the statement. *PRINT THE LETTER OF THE CORRECT ANSWER IN THE SPACE AT THE RIGHT.*

Questions 1-7.

DIRECTIONS: Questions 1 through 7 are to be answered SOLELY on the basis of the following rules. These rules are not intended to be an exact copy of the rules of any institution.

SECTION OF RULES

All members of the department shall treat as confidential the official business of the department. An employee shall under no circumstances impart information to anyone relating to the official business of the department, except when she is a witness under oath in a court of law. When answering a department telephone, an employee shall give the name of the institution to which she is attached, her rank, and full name. Officers shall not give the name of any bondsman or attorney to inmates. The head of the institution shall be notified immediately when an inmate requests an officer for the name of a bondsman or attorney. All inmates awaiting trial shall be advised that they are entitled to one free telephone call within the city. All other telephone calls must be paid for by the inmate. Officers assigned to the examination of parcels or letters for inmates shall do so with utmost care. Failure to discover contraband shall be presumptive evidence of negligence. When an officer is assigned to accompany an inmate to court, to the District Attorney's office, or elsewhere, she must handcuff the inmate and must, under no circumstances, visit any places except such as are designated in the document calling for the inmate's presence.

1. Assume that Mary Jones is assigned to the House of Detention as a Correction Officer with shield number 781.
   When she answers the institution's phone, she should say
   A. House of Detention, Officer Mary Jones
   B. House of Detention, Officer Mary Jones, shield number 781
   C. Officer Mary Jones, shield number 781
   D. This is the House of Detention, Officer Jones speaking

   1.____

2. An inmate awaiting trial asks for permission to make a telephone call to New Jersey.
   She should be
   A. allowed to make the call if she has not made any other free calls
   B. permitted to make the call at her own expense
   C. told that only local telephone calls are permitted
   D. told that she will have to pay all charges

   2.____

3. An inmate awaiting trial asks you for the name of a lawyer who will not charge a large fee, as she does not have much money.
   You should
   A. bring her request to the attention of the head of the institution
   B. remind her that under the rules inmates are forbidden to ask an officer for the name of an attorney
   C. tell her that you don't know any lawyers who charge low fees
   D. tell her the state will furnish a lawyer without charge

3._____

4. A supervisor has an inmate whose case received a great deal of publicity in the newspapers. One day a reporter comes to the supervisor's home to interview him about this prisoner.
   The supervisor should
   A. give him only such information as has already appeared in the daily press
   B. give him only such information which is not considered confidential
   C. tell him that he is prohibited by the rules from discussing the case with him
   D. tell him that an interview will be granted if he can produce a letter from the Commissioner giving him permission for the interview

4._____

5. An officer is assigned to deliver a prisoner to the hospital prison ward in accordance with a court order. He is given a department car and chauffeur for this purpose. Before he leaves, the Superintendent of the prison also gives him some important official papers requiring the Commissioner's immediate attention for delivery to Central Office. On the way to the hospital, he will pass Central Office.
   He should stop at Central Office
   A. and send the chauffeur in with the papers while he waits in the car with the prisoner
   B. on his way back from the hospital, after he has delivered his prisoner
   C. to deliver the papers, leaving the handcuffed prisoner in the car in charge of the chauffeur
   D. to deliver the papers, taking the handcuffed prisoner with him

5._____

6. According to the rules, if an article of contraband is successfully smuggled into the prison in a package for an inmate, it is
   A. possible that the contraband may have been extremely well concealed
   B. possible that the employee who inspected the package did not realize that the article in question constituted contraband
   C. probable that the employee who inspected the package was careless
   D. sufficient cause to make the employee who inspected the package subject to dismissal

6._____

7. According to the rules,
   A. an employee may testify about official business in court
   B. only a competent court or the District Attorney can order a prisoner to be produced

7._____

C. sentenced inmates are not allowed to make telephone calls out of the institution
D. while packages for inmates are censored, their personnel mail is not

Questions 8-11.

DIRECTIONS: Questions 8 through 11 are to be answered SOLELY on the basis of the following passage.

Female criminality is very much under-reported, especially if one considers offenses such as shoplifting, thefts by prostitutes, offenses against children, and homicide. There are even certain offenses such as homosexuality and exhibitionism that go practically unprosecuted if committed by women. Female offenders are really protected by men, even by victims, who are usually disinclined to complain to authorities. Since women play much less active role in society than men do, one must be prepared for the fact that women are often the instigators of crimes committed by men and, as instigators, they are hard to detect. There are several crimes that are ordinarily highly detectable in men but have very low detectability in women. Her roles as homemaker, mother, nurse, wife, and so forth, permit the female to commit a crime and yet screen that crime from public view—for example, slowly poisoning her husband or treating her children abusively. In addition, law enforcement officers, judges, and juries are much more lenient toward women than toward men. Such considerations lead to the conclusion that criminality of women is *largely masked criminality*. Consequently, official statistics and records of criminality should be expected to under-report female offenses. The true measure of female crime must be sought from unofficial sources. The masked character of female crime and its gross under-reporting are consistent with the official view that the female is a very low risk for crime.

8. What has the writer inferred about the incidence of female offenses?
    A. It gives an adequate representation of the number of crimes committed by men but instigated by women.
    B. It is not to be considered an important area of criminality.
    C. It is understated because the classic female role makes her less visible to social scrutiny.
    D. In every crime the incidence of male offenses is more difficult than that of women.

9. Judges are inclined to be lenient toward female offenders because
    A. the role of the woman in society has stereotyped her as maternal and non-hostile
    B. the majority of their crimes does not physically harm others
    C. they commit crimes which are difficult to detect
    D. official statistics report them as less likely to commit crimes

10. Of the following, the title MOST suitable for this passage is
    A. Male Criminality
    B. The Petty Offender
    C. The Female Murderer
    D. Exposing Female Criminality

11. According to the passage, which of the following crimes is LEAST likely to be prosecuted against a woman? 11.____
    A. Child abuse
    B. Exhibitionism
    C. Homicide
    D. Prostitution

Questions 12-16.

DIRECTIONS: Questions 12 through 16 are to be answered SOLELY on the basis of the following passage. Each of the questions consist of two statements. Read the passage carefully, and then mark your answer
A. if both statements are correct according to the information given in the passage
B. if both statements are incorrect according to the information given in the passage
C. if one statement is correct and one is incorrect according to the information given in the passage
D. if the correctness or incorrectness of one or both of the statements cannot be determined from the information given in the passage.

The twentieth century has opened to women many pursuits from which they were formerly excluded and thus has given them new opportunities for crime. Can we assume that as a result of this development female crime will change its nature and become like masculine crime through losing its masked character? In periods of pronounced social stress, such as war, in which women assume many roles otherwise open only to men, experience indicates that crimes of women against property increase. Can we assume, further, that simultaneously the amount of undiscovered female crime decreases? Further study contradicts the validity of this assumption. Their new roles have become wage earners and household heads, but they have not stopped being the homemakers, the rearers of children, the nurses, or the shoppers. With the burden of their social functions increased, their opportunities for crime have not undergone a process of substitution so much as a process of increase.

12. I. As women assumed increased social burdens, there was a marked change in the character of their opportunities for crime. 12.____
    II. Although the crimes committed by women have increased, they are still fewer in number than those committed by men.

13. I. Male crime is less masked in character than female crime. 13.____
    II. The opportunities of women to commit crimes have increased in the last fifty years.

14. I. In wartime, when they have increased employment opportunities, women commit fewer crimes against property. 14.____
    II. When the social equality of women increases, the number of undetected crimes which they commit decreases.

15. I. In the period between 1900 and 1968, women did not gain many new opportunities for employment. 15.____
    II. In a family unit, the role of the shopper is traditionally that of the wife rather than that of the husband.

16. I. The crime rate increases in periods of social stress, such as war.
    II. Because women have not wanted to be limited to their traditional roles of homemaker and rearer of children, they have sought social equality with men.

Questions 17-18.

DIRECTIONS: Questions 1 through 6 are to be answered SOLELY on the basis of the following passage.

The public has become increasingly aware that rehabilitation that great battle cry of prison reform is one of the great myths of twentieth century penology. The hard truth is that punishment and retribution are the primary, if not the only, functions served by most correctional institutions. Courts can provide enlightened rule-making to assist prison reform and ombudsmen can give prisoners a forum to consider their complaints but the results would be limited. The corrections system will never run with any real efficiency until: (a) prisoners want to be reformed; (b) prison administrators want to help them reform; (c) courts want to help both toward a system of reform; and (d) they all define reform in the same way. If this is not done, the criminal justice system will continue to operate on the model of concentric layers of coercion, a grossly inefficient model.

17. According to the above passage, all of the following will be required in order to improve the correction system EXCEPT
    A. commitment to reform by prison administrators
    B. development by penal experts of criteria for meaningful rehabilitation
    C. acceptance by prisoners of the need for their cooperation
    D. assistance by the courts in providing a system where reform is possible

18. According to the above passage, meaningful prison reform is MOST likely to result from
    A. the appointment of ombudsmen to replace the courts in ruling on prisoners' complaints
    B. coordination by sociologists of efforts to improve prison conditions
    C. a realization by society that rehabilitation of prisoners is no longer a realistic objective
    D. the joint efforts of those directly concerned and a common understanding of the goals to be achieved

Questions 19-25.

DIRECTIONS: Each of Questions 19 through 25 begins with a statement. Your answer to each of these questions MUST be based only upon this statement and not on any other information you may have.

19. At any given moment, the number of people coming out of prisons in the United States is substantially as great as the number entering them.
    Of the following, the MOST reasonable assumption on the basis of the preceding statement is that

A. most prisoners in the United States are recidivists
B. the crime rate in this country is decreasing
C. the crime rate in this country is increasing
D. the prison population of this country is constant

20. The indeterminate sentence usually sets a lower limit for the time to be served, and an upper limit. In some cases, there is a maximum limit, but no minimum; in some, a minimum but no maximum; and in others, neither a maximum nor a minimum, the time to be served being determined by the prisoner's conduct and other considerations.
In the preceding statement, the one of the following which is NOT given as a characteristic of the indeterminate sentence is that
    A. sometimes the maximum time which must be served is not set at the time of sentence
    B. sometimes the minimum time which must be served is not set at the time of sentence
    C. the exact length of time to be served is fixed at the time of sentence
    D. the length of time to be served may vary with the prisoner's behavior

21. Overcrowding in a prison makes segregation of prisoners more difficult, complicates the maintenance of order and discipline, and endangers health and morals.
Of the following, the MOST reasonable assumption based on the preceding statement is that
    A. if prisoners are allowed to associate too freely their health and morals will be endangered
    B. in a prison that is not overcrowded there will not be any problems of order and discipline
    C. it is undesirable for the inmate population to exceed unduly the intended capacity of a prison
    D. segregation of prisoners is carried on mainly for the purpose of better prison administration

22. Most non-professional shoplifters are women of comfortable means who could buy the things they steal.
Of the following, the MOST valid conclusion which can be drawn from the preceding statement is that
    A. some well-to-do women are shoplifters
    B. most professional shoplifters are men
    C. few women practice shoplifting as a profession
    D. most shoplifters suffer from a mental ailment rather than from a moral deficiency

23. Since accomplices and instigators are harder to detect and successfully prosecute than overt perpetrators, most women offenders therefore escape punishment.
Of the following, the MOST valid conclusion which can be drawn from the preceding statement is that

A. judges deal more leniently with females than with male offenders
B. men who are accomplices or instigators of crimes are easier to detect and prosecute than woman
C. successful prosecution of women offenders depends to a large extent on their successful detection
D. women are more often accomplices in, rather than actual perpetrators of, criminal acts

24. Through the juvenile court, the recognition of social responsibility in the delinquent acts of an individual has been established.
The MOST accurate of the following statements on the basis of the preceding statement is that
    A. delinquent behavior is an evidence of an individual's social irresponsibility
    B. some individuals are responsible for their delinquent acts
    C. the juvenile court is evidence of society's willingness to assume some blame for the anti-social behavior of its younger members
    D. the juvenile court takes into consideration the age, social background, and offense of the individual before deciding upon his punishment

24._____

25. The way to win more offenders to lasting good behavior is to provide treatment to each offender based on an understanding of the causes of his actions and of his emotional needs in the light of modern insight into human nature.
Of the following, the MOST valid inference which can be drawn from the preceding statement is that
    A. few offenders are reformed today because they are not led to an understanding of the causes of their criminal actions
    B. individualized attention is required to achieve reform in criminals
    C. penologists have a better understanding of the causes of criminal behavior because of recent developments in the study of human nature
    D. unsolved emotional conflicts frequently result in criminal acts

25._____

KEY (CORRECT ANSWERS)

1.	A	11.	B
2.	B	12.	D
3.	A	13.	A
4.	C	14.	B
5.	B	15.	C
6.	C	16.	D
7.	A	17.	B
8.	C	18.	D
9.	A	19.	D
10.	D	20.	C

21.	C
22.	A
23.	D
24.	C
25.	B

MYTHS AND REALITIES ABOUT CRIME

CONTENTS

	Page
ABOUT NATIONAL CRIME TRENDS	1
ABOUT THE EXTENT OF VIOLENT CRIME	1
ABOUT CRIME IN BIG CITIES	2
ABOUT POLICE PERFORMANCE	2
ABOUT REPORTING CRIME	3
ABOUT MINORITIES AND THE POLICE	3
ABOUT NEIGHBORHOOD PROBLEMS	4
ABOUT NEIGHBORHOOD SAFETY	4
ABOUT FEAR OF CRIME	5
ABOUT CRIME AGAINST THE ELDERLY	5
ABOUT CRIME AGAINST WOMEN	6
ABOUT ARMED VIOLENCE	6
ABOUT WEAPONS AND INJURIES	7
ABOUT USING FORCE FOR SELF-DEFENSE	7
ABOUT VICTIM INJURY	8
ABOUT THE CLASSIC HOLD-UP	8
ABOUT RESIDENTIAL BURGLARS	8
ABOUT VICTIM-OFFENDER RELATIONSHIPS	9
ABOUT SERIOUS ASSAULT BY STRANGERS	9
ABOUT THE CRIMINAL AS A LONER	10
ABOUT DRUGS AND CRIME	10
ABOUT UNEMPLOYMENT AND CRIME	11

MYTHS AND REALITIES ABOUT CRIME

About national crime trends

Myth
Crime in the Nation is rising by leaps and bounds.

Reality
The incidence of certain major crimes of violence and common theft is just about keeping pace with population growth.

A strong degree of stability characterized the rate at which the American people, as well as their homes and businesses, were victimized by the selected offenses measured by the National Crime Survey (NCS). Year-to-year fluctuations in victimization rates were relatively small, even when statistically significant, and an overall trend had yet to form. Although additional confirmation is needed, the possibility is provocative that crime, like other measurable human activity, undergoes change in a gradual, undramatic way. It cannot be overlooked, however, that the volume of NCS-measured crime was high — averaging an estimated 39.9 million victimizations per year, including about 5.8 million violent offenses.

About the extent of violent crime

Myth
Most crimes measured as taking place in the United States are of a violent nature.

Reality
Of the NCS-measured offenses, the vast majority are against property only and do not involve personal violence or threat.

Although the National Crime Survey gauges the occurrence of but a limited number of types of offenses, those involving violence — rape, personal or commercial robbery, and assault — made up **only about 14 percent** of the total volume of crime measured. Larceny of personal or household property was the most common crime, accounting for some 62 percent of those measured. About one-fifth of the offenses were burglaries, most of them residential, and the remainder (3 percent) were motor vehicle thefts. It must be pointed out, however, that two major violent crimes, homicide and kidnaping, are not addressed by the NCS and that the program was not designed to measure a variety of property offenses, including white collar crimes and commercial larcenies.

About crime in big cities

Myth
The larger the city, the greater the likelihood that its residents will be the victims of crime.

Reality
For certain crimes, the residents of smaller cities have higher rates than those of our largest cities.

The rates of assault, personal or household larceny, and residential burglary have tended to be relatively lower for people living in our largest cities (i.e., 1 million or more population) than for those residing in smaller cities. Personal robbery rates, however, have been higher among the residents of the largest cities, and the occurrence of motor vehicle theft has been **more pronounced** for households located in cities of 1/2 million or more inhabitants than in smaller ones. Cities in the 1/2 to 1 million population range have evidenced a relatively high household burglary rate.

About police performance

Myth
In general, residents of large cities believe their police are doing a poor job.

Reality
If the opinions of residents of numerous cities across the Nation are indicative, the vast majority is satisfied with the performance of their police.

When asked if their local police were doing a good, average, or poor job, some **four of every five** residents of 26 cities surveyed gave ratings **of good or average**. Those who characterized the police work in that manner accounted for approximately 17.2 million of the estimated 21.1 million person's age 16 and over living in those cities. Some 2.5 million rated the police as poor, and 1.4 million had no opinion on the matter. Each of the 26 localities surveyed had a total population of 100,000 or more, and the group included the Nation's nine largest cities. Combined, the 26 cities had an estimated population of about 28.6 million. The interviews, however, were taken only among persons age 16 and over, and half the cities were surveyed.

About reporting crime

Myth
Most crime is reported to the police.

Reality
Slightly fewer than half of all offenses measured by the National Crime Survey are known to the police.

Although the rate at which victims report crimes to the police has varied widely depending on the type or seriousness of the crime, less than a third of personal offenses and only 38 percent of household incidents were made known to the police. These relatively low overall rates of reporting can be ascribed in part to the prevalence of larceny—the least well reported of crimes—among offenses against individuals or residences. Burglary or robbery of businesses, together with motor vehicle theft, have had the highest police reporting rates. Of all crimes measured by the National Crime Survey during the 4-year period, some 48 percent were reported to the police. Whether incurred by individuals, households, or businesses, the more serious forms of crime generally were more likely to be reported; because of space limitations, however, the accompanying chart distinguishes two forms of seriousness only for assault.

About minorities and the police

Myth
Blacks or Hispanics are less likely than the population as a whole to report personal crimes to the police.

Reality
By and large, the offenses experienced by members of those two minority groups are just about as apt to be reported as are crimes against victims in general.

The rates at which black victims reported personal crimes of violence, whether the offenses are considered collectively or individually, as well as personal crimes of theft (i.e., larcenies), did **not differ** significantly from the corresponding rates for the population at large. Similar findings applied to the reporting of crimes by victims of Hispanic ancestry, except with respect to personal robberies or larcenies, which Hispanics were slightly **less likely** than victims in general to report to the police.

About neighborhood problems

Myth

The residents of our large cities regard crime as the most important neighborhood problem.

Reality

Judging from the opinions of many city residents, environmental problems cause just about as much concern as crime.

"Is there anything you don't like about this neighborhood?" This question was asked of persons representing about 10.1 million households in 26 large cities across the Nation. Only 38 percent answered "yes." These individuals, representatives for some 3.8 million households, were then asked what they disliked **most** about their neighborhoods. The two largest groups (26 percent each) felt that **crime or environmental deterioration**—trash, noise, overcrowding, and the like—were the main problems. Fourteen percent of the residents said they were displeased with their neighbors. Miscellaneous problems, none of them exceeding about one-tenth of all responses, were cited by the remainder. It must be remembered, however, that a majority of the individuals surveyed found no fault with their neighborhoods.

About neighborhood safety

Myth

Most residents of large cities think their neighborhoods are not safe.

Reality

Most individuals feel at least reasonably safe when out alone in their neighborhoods either in the daytime or at night.

Nine in every ten persons living in 26 large cities surveyed felt **very** or **reasonably safe** when out alone in their neighborhoods during daytime. Considerably fewer, although still a majority (54 percent), felt similarly with respect to nighttime. Concerning daytime conditions, "very safe" responses were the most prevalent, accounting for 48 percent, whereas "reasonably safe" was the most commonplace answer to the question about nighttime. Only 3 percent of the residents said they were very **unsafe** when out alone in their vicinity during the day, but about seven times that number felt likewise about nighttime.

About fear of crime

Myth
Most residents of large cities have limited or changed their activities because of the fear of crime.

Reality
If the assessments of an estimated 21.1 million persons are indicative, slightly fewer than half of all big-city residents have personally altered their lifestyles because of crime.

The belief that city people have had to modify their daily activities because of the threat of crime is widespread, even among city dwellers themselves. The results of attitude surveys conducted in 26 cities suggest, however, that this opinion does not necessarily translate into a curtailment in personal activities. A **vast majority** of the residents of those cities thought that crime had caused "people in general" to limit or change their activities in recent years. Most (63 percent) also believed that the residents of their own neighborhood had done so. For themselves personally, however, **46 percent** indicated they had altered their lifestyles. A slight majority was of the opinion that crime had not affected their lifestyles.

About crime against the elderly

Myth
Elderly persons make up the most heavily victimized age group in our society.

Reality
Rates of victimization are far higher for young individuals than for senior citizens.

The National Crime Survey has demonstrated repeatedly that the elderly (age 65 and over) are the victims of personal crime, whether involving violence or theft only, at rates **far lower** than young individuals (age 12-24). The rates for residential crimes among households headed by elderly persons have also been **comparatively** low. These findings, however, ignore the trauma and economic burden brought about by crime, which no doubt weigh more heavily on elderly victims than on young ones. The lower rates among the elderly may relate to precautionary measures taken and/or to self-imposed isolation designed to minimize exposure to threatening situations. NCS attitude surveys conducted in 26 cities revealed that senior citizens were **more likely** than younger persons to indicate they had modified their activities because of **fear of crime**. Well over half the estimated 3.2 million persons age 65 and over living in those cities said they had done so.

About crime against women

Myth
Women are more likely than men to be the victims of crime.

Reality
For various personal crimes, men are victimized at higher rates than women.

For personal robbery or assault, as well as for personal larceny without victim-offender contact, men have been victimized at **appreciably higher** rates than women. With respect to the two violent crimes, men had **consistently higher** victimization rates than women for cases in which the victim and offender were strangers to one another. Also, men were **somewhat likelier** than women to have experienced assaults at the hands of nonstrangers. Aside from rape, the only NCS-measured personal crime having a **higher** rate for women was larceny with contact (i.e., purse snatchings and pocket pickings); however, the rate differences for this class of crime have been nominal, if not statistically insignificant.

About armed violence

Myth
A weapon is used by the offender in nearly all rapes, robberies, and assaults.

Reality
Weapons are used in far fewer than half all those crimes.

Of the three violent personal crimes measured by the National Crime Survey, rape was the least likely and robbery was the most likely to have been perpetrated by armed offenders. With 35 percent of all incidents involving an offender who used a weapon, assault ranked in between the other two personal crimes. On the other hand, an average of **71 percent** of all robberies of businesses during the 4-year period involved armed encounters. Because of the prevalence of personal crimes of violence, however, the average for all four of these crimes taken together was **39 percent**.

About weapons and injuries

Myth
A victim is more likely to be injured during an armed assault or robbery if the offender wields a firearm rather than a knife or other weapon.

Reality
The victim's likelihood of sustaining injury at the hands of an armed offender is lessened if the weapon is a firearm.

In the course of either an aggravated assault or personal robbery by an armed offender, the likelihood of victim injury has been **greatest** when the crime was carried out with the aid of an object **other than a firearm or knife**, such as a club, brick, wrench, or bottle. The presence of a knife, as opposed to a firearm, has also been associated with a higher incidence of victim injury. These findings, based on National Crime Survey data, suggest that victims are less apt to resist a criminal armed with a lethal weapon and, therefore, are less likely to be injured. It must be pointed out, however, that as presently constituted, the NCS makes no determination of the actual **cause of injury**; therefore, the accompanying chart should not be construed to represent the percentage of incidents in which victims were harmed by the weapons listed. Also, the program does **not measure kidnaping** or violent crimes resulting in **death**, for which the relationships among types of weapons may differ from those portrayed for assault and personal robbery.

About using force for self-defense

Myth
People often use force or weapons for self-defense from criminal attack.

Reality
Although victims defend themselves in a majority of rapes, robberies, or assaults, passive methods are more commonly used for protection.

Victims took some measure of self-protection in about **two-thirds** of the personal crimes of violence (i.e., rapes, robberies, and assaults) that occurred. They were most apt to have done so in cases of rape and least likely in those of robbery. The likelihood of employing self-defense did not, however, differ markedly if the encounters were between strangers or nonstrangers. Only with respect to robbery were the victims appreciably less likely to defend themselves in stranger-to-stranger confrontations than in cases involving nonstrangers. Although a substantial number of victims employed **physical means** of resistance, such as striking the offender (29 percent) or using a gun or knife (2 percent), far more resorted to a variety of **passive methods**—sought help, ran away, hid, ducked, reasoned with the offender, and so forth (58 percent).

About victim injury

Myth
More often than not, the victims of violent crimes other than homicide end up in a hospital.

Reality
Relatively few victims of rape, robbery, or assault get hospital care, either in an emergency room or as inpatients.

In only **8 percent** of personal crimes of violence (i.e., rape, robbery, and assault considered collectively) that happened during, the victims were treated in hospitals. Of those treated, 24 percent obtained inpatient care, whereas the majority received emergency room treatment and were released. Among those hospitalized as inpatients, victims were somewhat more likely to be confined for 4 or more days than for a shorter period.

About the classic hold-up

Myth
The typical personal robbery is carried out against a lone pedestrian by an armed offender operating alone.

Reality
Although the victim is usually alone and outdoors, the robber does not necessarily work alone or use a weapon.

While it is true that the vast bulk of personal robberies happened to lone victims and most took place on streets or other outdoor places, about half of the incidents committed were by two or more offenders, many of whom did not employ a weapon. In fact, unarmed robberies took place just about as often as armed robberies, and the presence of a weapon was somewhat more likely in multiple-offender incidents than in those involving offenders who operated alone.

About residential burglars

Myth
Household burglars usually commit their crimes by breaking into the premises.

Reality
In a majority of completed residential burglaries committed throughout the United States, burglars gain entry into homes or apartments without resorting to force.

Most burglars are successfully carrying out their crimes **simply by entering** through unlocked doors or windows, or by using keys. Some 57 percent of all completed household burglaries that took place were unlawful entries **without force**, whereas the remainder was forcible entries. Probably as a result of a greater concern for household security on the part of urban dwellers, burglaries of central city or suburban residences were more likely than those in nonmetropolitan places to have been break-ins.

About victim-offender relationships

Myth
　　The victims of crime seldom know or recognize their offenders.

Reality
　　A substantial number of crimes are committed by persons known to their victims.

　　In **35 percent** of the estimated **22** million rapes, personal robberies, or assaults that took place, the victims were acquainted with, if not related to, the offenders. It is reasonable to assume, moreover, that many more crimes (especially assaults) by nonstrangers were **not revealed** to National Crime Survey interviewers. In addition, attitude surveys conducted in 26 large cities showed that an average of **36 percent** of persons victimized in the preceding year believed that neighborhood crime was being committed either by persons living within the vicinity or by insiders and outsiders alike. Nevertheless, the largest number of residents attributed crime to offenders from outside the neighborhood, and one-fourth did not know where the culprits came from. Only 3 percent indicated their neighborhoods were free of crime.

About serious assaults by strangers

Myth
　　Aggravated assaults are more likely to result in physical injury if the attacker is a total stranger.

Reality
　　One's chances of being injured and ending up in a hospital are somewhat greater if the assailant is not a stranger.

　　Of the estimated 2.4 million aggravated assaults committed by friends, casual acquaintances, or relatives, some **38 percent** resulted in physical injury to the victims. This compares with a **30 percent** injury rate for the 4.3 million crimes in which the assailants were strangers. The higher injury rate among the victims of nonstrangers applied to men and women, as well as to whites. Women, in particular, were **more likely** to be injured by nonstranger than by strangers. There was no statistically significant difference between the two injury rates for black victims. As suggested by hospitalization rates for the victims of aggravated assault, moreover, persons attacked by nonstrangers probably sustained **serious injuries** relatively more often than those who experienced stranger-to-stranger offenses. The hospitalization rate for the latter was some 5 percentage points lower.

About the criminal as a loner

Myth
The typical prison inmate is a "loner" with no family or friends and little social contact.

Reality
Perhaps because most had lived in a family situation prior to their arrest, prisoners are quite likely to maintain regular social contacts during incarceration.

Although some inmates of State correctional facilities fit the stereotype of the "social misfit," devoid of family ties or friendships, most appear to have had social relationships both before arrest and during imprisonment. Some three-fifths of all inmates questioned about their living arrangements **had lived with family** members before the arrest; indeed, many were **supporting** relatives, or others, besides themselves. Once in prison, 46 percent of all sentenced inmates were being visited by family and/or friends at least monthly, 26 percent had less frequent visits, and only 27 percent never saw outsiders. The vast majority of sentenced inmates — some 87 percent — maintained regular communication by telephone or letter with relatives or acquaintances; this group included roughly 64 percent who had such contacts at least once a week and 23 percent at least once a month. An additional 7 percent had less frequent external contacts.

About drugs and crime

Myth
People are usually under the influence of drugs when they commit a crime.

Reality
If the experience of those imprisoned for all types of offenses is indicative, the occurrence of most crime cannot be attributed to drug-induced aberrant behavior.

A **majority** of the inmates of State correctional facilities were **not under the influence** of drugs (other than alcohol) when committing the crimes, whether against persons or property, that led to their incarceration. Roughly 1 in 4 of these inmates had been under the influence of some type of drug. Of those who **had been on drugs**, 36 percent (or one-tenth of the total) said they had been using heroin exclusively at the time of the offense. An equal proportion had been under the influence of one other drug, such as marijuana, amphetamines, or barbiturates. The remaining inmates had been using a combination of two or more drugs.

About unemployment and crime

Myth
The typical person who commits a crime is either unemployed or on welfare.

Reality
Based on what is known about imprisoned criminals, most persons who engage in crime have jobs and very few are welfare-dependent.

State correctional facilities were not populated chiefly by the unemployed or indigent. On the contrary, roughly two-thirds of the inmates had **held jobs**, the bulk of them on a full-time basis, during the month before their arrest. Twelve percent had **sought** employment during that period, whereas 19 percent were **not looking for** jobs, either because they did not want to or could not work. As for the main source of income during the year prior to incarceration, some 77 percent of the inmates lived mainly off **wages or salaries**. Only 3 percent had been dependent upon welfare assistance. It should be pointed out, however, that among inmates who had income from any source, the median amount was relatively low — only $14,630. This figure was about **45 percent lower** than the median for all income-earning males age 14 and over, the group in the general population most nearly comparable with the inmate population.